£6.50

D0245874

history at s

THE EDWARDIAN

AGE *1901-1914*

Vyvyen Brendon

Hodder & Stoughton

ACKNOWLEDGEMENTS

I am grateful to my past and present sixth-form pupils at St Mary's School, Cambridge, who have studied many of these sources and stimulated me with their lively responses.

The publishers wish to thank the following for permission to reproduce illustrations in this volume: Cover - *Gala Day at Newlyn* by Stanhope Forbes, courtesy of Hartelpool Museum Service.
Daily Herald, p. 9; Liberal Party archives p. 25; Mary Evans Picture Library, p. 28; courtesy of The Salvation Army International Heritage Centre p. 45; Nature Conservancy Council, p. 52; Conservative Party archives/Fotomas Index, p. 55; The Labour Party, p. 62; Museum of London, p. 74; Fotomas Index, p. 75; National Library of Scotland/courtesy of the author, p. 84; the Ulster Museum, Belfast, p. 85; Fotomas Index, p. 95; Scouts Association, p. 99; Dorest Local History Reference Library, p. 108; Hulton-Deutsch Picture Library, p. 112.
Every effort has been made to trace and acknowledge ownership of copyright. The publishers will be glad to make suitable arrangements with any copyright holders whom it has not been possible to contact.

Text acknowledgements page iv

British Library Cataloguing in Publication Data

A catalogue for this title is available from the British Library

ISBN 0 340 63086 8

First published 1996
Impression number   10 9 8 7 6 5 4 3 2 1
Year   1999 1998 1997 1996

Typeset by Sempringham publishing services, Bedford
Printed in Great Britain for Hodder and Stoughton Educational, a division of Hodder Headline Plc, 338 Euston Road, London NW1 3BH by Redwood Books, Trowbridge

CONTENTS

Text acknowledgements

The publishers would like to thank the following for their permission to reproduce material in this volume: Blackwell Publishers for the extracts from S Humphries, *Hooligans or Rebels: An Oral History of Working-Class Childhood and Youth* (1981); B T Batsford Ltd for extracts from M Bruce, *The Coming of the Welfare State* (1965); Blackstaff Press Ltd for extracts from the Report on the Loss of the Titanic (1990); Charles Knight Publishing for extracts from R Frow, E Frow and M Katanka, *Strikes* (1971); Cambridge University Press for extraxts from R Blake, *Bonar Law - The Unknown Prime Minister* (1955); Curtis Brown for extracts from Marchioness Curzon of Kedleston, *Reminicences* (1955); David and Charles Publishers for extracts from N McCord, *Free Trade* (1970); Everyman for extracts from H G Wells, *Kipps* (1993); Faber and Faber Ltd for extracts from E Howard, *Garden Cities of Tomorrow* (1965), A T Q Stewart, *The Ulster Crisis* (1967), P Larkin, *Whitsun Weddings* (1964); Robert Hale Ltd for extracts from A Ross, *Reverie* (1981); Harrap for extracts from D Read, *Edwardian England* (1972), D Read, *Documents From Edwardian England* (1973); HarperCollins Publishers for extracts from E Royston, *Human Documents of the Lloyd George Era* (1972), L Baily, *BBC Scrapbook 1900-1914* (1966), P Kennedy, *The Rise and Fall of the Great Powers* (1989), F S Lyons, *Ireland Since the Famine* (1989), R Tressell, *The Ragged Trousered Philanthropist* (1993), T Wilson, *The Downfall of the Liberal Party* (1989), G Dangerfield, *The Strange Death of Liberal England* (1966); Harvester Wheatsheaf for extracts from A White, *Efficiency and Empire* (1973), P Jalland, *The Liberals and Ireland* (1980); William Heinemann for extracts from L Butler and H Jones, *Britain in the Twentieth Century: A Documentary Reader* (1994), R Jenkins, *Mr Balfour's Poodle* (1968), B Catchpole, *A Map History of the Modern World* (1982); Longman Group Ltd for extracts from ed. M Cole, *The Diaries of Beatrice Webb* (1952), P Adelman, *The Rise of the Labour Party* (1972), P Wardley, *Edwardian Britain* a chapter from *Twentieth Century Britain* ed. P Johnson (1984), D Read, *The Age of Urban Democracy* (1994), D Vincent, *Poor Citizens* (1991); Macmillan General Books for extracts from H G Wells, *Tono-Bungay* (1964), R Jenkins, *Asquith* (1994), ed. O'Day, *The Political Economy in Edwardian England* a chapter from *The Edwardian Age* (1979), D Butler and J Freeman, *British Political Facts* (1963), S O'Casey, *Drums Under the Windows* (1945), B Tuchmann, *August 1914* (1980); Methuen for extracts from G Sowerby, *Rutherford and Son* (1994), E Curtis and R McDowell, *Irish Historical Documents* (1990), ed. B Gardner, *Up to the Line of Death* (1976); Oxford University Press for extracts from L T Hobhouse, *Liberalism* (1963), R McKibbin, *The Evolution of the Labour Party* (1974), E Blunden, *Country Childhood from Edwardian England*, ed. S Nowell-Smith (1963), R C K Ensor, *England 1870-1914* (1936); Penguin Books Ltd for extracts from J Barrie, *Peter Pan* (1994), J P Taylor, *The First World War* (1963), V Sackville-West, *The Edwardians* (1990), G B Shaw, *Man and Superman* (1946), M Girouard, *Life in the English Country House* (1978), V S Pritchett, *A Cab at the Door* and *Midnight Oil* (1979), G B Shaw, *John Bull's Other Island* (1984), R Graves, *Goodbye to All That* (1960); Random House UK Ltd. for extracts from L Woolf, *Beginning Again* (1968), L Tickner, *The Spectacle of Women* (1992), P Addison, *Churchill on the Home Front* (1992); Routledge for extracts from D Read ed., *Edwardian England* (1982), P Thompson, *The Edwardians* (1992), T Thompson, *Edwardian Childhoods* (1981), E Evans, *Social Policy 1830-1914* (1978), C McPhee, *The Non-Violent Militant* (1987); Secker and Warburg for extracts from R Whitehouse, *A London Album* (1980), W S Adams, *Edwardian Portraits* (1957); Thomas Nelson & Sons Ltd for extracts from S Rowntree and M Kendall, *How the Labourer Lives* (1913); Victor Gallancz Ltd for extracts from V Brittain, *Testament of Youth* (1933); Virago Press for extracts from M Pember Reeves, *Round About a Pound a Week*, H G Wells, *Ann Veronica* (1980), G Gissing, *The Odd Women* (1980), S Pankhurst, *The Suffragette Movement* (1977).

Every effort has been made to trace and acknowledge ownership of copyright. The publishers will be glad to make suitable arrangements with any copyright holders whom it has not been possible to contact.

APPROACHING SOURCE-BASED

QUESTIONS

This book aims to provide a set of key documents illustrating the Edwardian Age from 1901 to 1914, and to suggest how the material can best be analysed and interpreted. Questions based on documents form a compulsory part of all A level history exam papers. Some boards include documentary questions in outline courses and all make them a dominant feature of depth studies. It is not unusual for as much as 50 per cent of the marks to be allocated to the document section. The questions vary; some require the study of prescribed texts, extracts from which appear on the exam paper for analysis. Others do not indicate specific texts but set detailed questions on documentary extracts that might not have been seen previously, but which candidates should be able to analyse by reference to their knowledge of the course.

Some questions test the candidate's ability to read and understand a historical document. Others examine background knowledge of wider themes or probe understanding of special topics. The most demanding are those which ask for evaluation of a historical document.

All papers indicate the marks on offer. These are a guide to the relative importance of the question and the proportion of time to be spent on it. As a rough rule of thumb, each mark offered should correspond to a point of fact or analysis. This should not be followed slavishly however; candidates can waste valuable time trying to find an extra point merely to satisfy an apparent numerical requirement.

Care should be taken to deal with the question as set. Examinees asked to evaluate a document will gain little from paraphrasing it or giving irrelevant details about its background. As well as showing understanding of sources, candidates at this level are expected to have an appreciation of historiography; that is, to know something about the problems in writing history. Being able to spot bias, attitude and motive in the writer of an extract is important. Questions requiring comment on the "tone" or the "colour" of a passage are common; and in responding to such questions, candidates should ask themselves: Does the writer seem angry, bitter, confident, detached, involved? Is the document an official report or a personal reminiscence? Does it suggest that it was written for a particular audience or is it a general statement? Is it propaganda or objective reporting? If candidates train themselves to do this, they will develop analytical skills that merit high marks.

1

INTRODUCTION

In an account of Queen Victoria's funeral, which took place in February 1901, the writer John Galsworthy described 'the coffin of the Age slowly passing'. The death of the old Queen, so soon after the turn of the century, prompted much comment about the new reign and the new era and how they would differ from the old. Some Edwardians, as subjects of King Edward VII soon dubbed themselves, believed with novelist H.G. Wells that 'the story of England' would soon reach its 'supreme dramatic moment'; others, like journalist J.L. Garvin, doubted whether England would 'last the century'. It seems that both optimists and pessimists got it wrong. This book examines the changes that actually did follow in the wake of the Victorian age.

There were no sharp changes in the way people lived. The deep 'cleavage of the classes' remained, with the poor becoming ever more conscious, and more resentful, of the wealth flaunted by landed and industrial magnates. Between these two poles the middle class gradually expanded, encompassing new professionals like teachers, civil servants and journalists. For all but the very poor, novel forms of transport and leisure made life more convenient and varied. Partly because of this, perhaps, religious observance steadily declined - to travel by motor-bus or tube-train to the cinema or a Cup Final might seem more exciting than regular attendance at church. The motor-car was still a luxury of the rich, of course, though the Prime Minister, Arthur Balfour, echoed the common view that it would 'help solve the congestion of traffic'. [Chapter 1.]

Parliament was still dominated by the great Victorian parties, the Liberals and the Conservatives, but both were worried by the arrival of cloth-capped MPs representing the new Labour Party. Neither the hopes of Labour's founders nor the fears of its opponents were fully realised in the Edwardian period. [Chapter 6.] However, its presence stimulated discussion about radical ways of tackling poverty and unemployment. The Liberal Party was especially receptive to such ideas, being anxious to maintain its appeal to the masses.

The Conservatives (or Unionists, as they were often called because of their opposition to Irish Home Rule) were discredited by the last painful stages of the Boer War (1899-1902). They were also split by Joseph Chamberlain's Tariff Reform campaign to restore duties on foreign imports and give preference to goods from the Empire. [Chapter 2.] After losing power to the Liberals in the landslide election of 1906, the Conservatives in opposition under Balfour (and later Andrew Bonar Law) clung to their traditional policies of defending private property and established institutions.

The first Liberal Prime Minister of the Edwardian age, Henry Campbell-

Bannerman, was cautiously progressive. After 1908 his successor, H.H. Asquith, fostered a 'new Liberalism', which included a degree of state intervention unthinkable in Gladstone's day. This took the form of welfare measures such as old age pensions, labour exchanges and even minimum wages in some trades. David Lloyd George and Winston Churchill were ardent champions of these reforms. [Chapter 4.]

Members of all parties were concerned about whether Britain would be able to uphold her position in the world against economic and military rivals. Their anxiety was sharpened by reports about the physical deficiencies of volunteers during the Boer War. Moreover, trade figures showed that Britain's industrial supremacy was being challenged by Germany and America. This led to a campaign for 'national efficiency', which attracted support from left and right - a new generation of 'effective citizens' must be created. Thus the Conservatives passed their 1902 Education Act and the Liberals began meals and medical inspections in schools - efforts to improve, respectively, the minds and the bodies of the nation's youth. Meanwhile, Baden-Powell's Boy Scout movement concentrated on the moral uplift of its recruits. [Chapter 3.]

As in Victorian times, the Liberals found some of their policies obstructed by the Conservative House of Lords, which still had the power to veto legislation. A series of skirmishes developed into a major conflict when, in 1909, the Lords rejected Lloyd George's 'People's Budget'. This introduced higher taxes (especially on the rich) to pay for social welfare and new battleships. The government was determined not to be thwarted by the unelected assembly. After two elections and a royal threat to create more Liberal peers, the Budget was passed - and so was the Parliament Act of 1911, which permanently limited the Lords' powers. [Chapter 5.]

In the midst of this constitutional crisis Edward VII died. His son, George V, came to the throne and was crowned to the patriotic strains of Elgar's Coronation March. Nevertheless, the years between 1910 and 1914 are usually included in the 'Edwardian era'. This is because so many developments straddled the two reigns but were harshly interrupted by the First World War. Despite difficulties, Liberal welfare policies continued. The National Insurance Act of 1911 was an attempt to provide a safety net to stop some workers from falling into poverty through unemployment or ill-health. The innovation was widely opposed; social reform was by no means always popular. [Chapter 4.]

This was not the only source of unrest in the late Edwardian years. Trade unionists were in a militant mood. They were dismayed by the Osborne judgement of 1909, which outlawed their financial support for the Labour Party. They were also dissatisfied with their standard of living, which was static if not actually falling. Strikes became so frequent and bitter that many politicians feared the approach of the revolution advocated by the extreme left, or 'syndicalist', wing of the labour movement. [Chapter 6.]

Edwardian tranquillity was also disturbed by the 'new women', who were determined to break free from their age-old subservience. Some defied fathers and husbands to pursue their education or careers and some dared also to defy the strict sexual mores of the day. The most militant crusaders were Mrs Pankhurst's suffragettes who, in their quest for the vote, resorted to shockingly violent methods. Whether these tactics made Parliament more or less disposed to grant their demands remains a matter of debate. [Chapter 7.]

The greatest threat to the internal peace of the kingdom came from Ireland. In 1912 the Liberals, who now depended on Irish support, introduced a new Home Rule bill. But during the two-year delay which the Lords still had the right to impose, the opposition of the Ulster Unionists and their Conservative allies hardened. It seemed that Home Rule could not be implemented without turmoil, perhaps even civil war. The bill had passed into law by July 1914 but, when war broke out in Europe, it was suspended. This was not to be the end of the story. [Chapter 8.]

Between 1910 and 1914 these various crises combined to create an atmosphere of discord. Civil strife in Ireland, a socialist revolution, a collapse of moral order - all seemed more likely to Edwardians than did Britain's participation in a world war. However, since the beginning of the century, amid growing international tensions, Britain had abandoned her so-called 'splendid isolation'. She had signed an alliance with Japan and forged friendly links with France and Russia. In response to weaknesses revealed by the Boer War and to Germany's increasing military and naval might, the Liberal government reorganised the army, strengthened the navy and made secret defence agreements with France. Meanwhile, several crises over rival imperial interests in Africa and the Balkans threatened to bring European countries to blows. Even so, most people were astonished when the assassination of Archduke Franz Ferdinand of Austria at Sarajevo started a train of events which led Britain to declare war on Germany in August 1914. Yet, the declaration was greeted with widespread public enthusiasm. [Chapter 9.]

Coming, as it did, before a horrific war, the Edwardian era has been the subject of much nostalgia and some controversy. Was it the sunlit age evoked by some writers? Or was it a time of tempestuous conflict? Did the Liberal Party weather the storms or was it struck down by the overwhelming forces of domestic unrest and the rising Labour Party? Should we view Edwardian Britain as an immature society which grew up during the war? Or had the country already moved into modern times? [Chapter 10.]

What we can certainly do, as we approach the end of this century, is to shed light on some of our problems by studying its early years. Economic decline, controversial taxation, ineradicable poverty, feminist claims, worries about decadent youth, Irish terrorism, armament races, even Balkan troubles - all are echoes from Edwardian times.

all concerns of today.

Chronology of the Edwardian Age

1900   Formation of the Labour Representation Committee
General ('khaki') election confirms Conservatives in power

1901   Death of Queen Victoria and accession of Edward VII
Taff Vale case threatens trade union funds

1902   Lord Salisbury resigns and Balfour becomes Prime Minister
Education Act
End of Boer War and Treaty of Vereeniging
Alliance with Japan

1903   Formation of Women's Social and Political Union
Visit of Edward VII to Paris
Chamberlain resigns and begins Tariff Reform campaign
Land Purchase Act for Ireland
Electoral pact between LRC and Liberal Party

1904   Licensing Act
Anglo-French Entente

1905   Tangier crisis
Appointment of Royal Commission on the Poor Law
Workmen's Compensation Act
Resignation of Conservative government

1906   General election results in Liberal victory
Campbell-Bannerman becomes Prime Minister
29 Labour MPs take their seats in Parliament
First Dreadnought launched
Algeciras Conference on future of Morocco
Trade Disputes Act reverses Taff Vale decision
Self-government granted to Boers
Beginning of law-breaking campaign by WSPU
Rejection of Education and Licensing Bills by Lords

1907   School meals service introduced
Haldane's army reforms
Split in WSPU
Anglo-Russian Entente
Beginning of Boy Scout movement

1908   Campbell-Bannerman resigns, Asquith becomes Prime Minister and
Lloyd George Chancellor of the Exchequer
Children's Charter
Old Age Pensions Act
Austrian annexation of Bosnia

1909   Poor Law Report
Labour exchanges introduced
Trade Boards Act

Osborne judgement
'People's Budget' passed in Commons and rejected in Lords
Formation of Women's Anti-Suffrage League
1910 General election returns Liberals to power with no overall majority
Churchill becomes Home Secretary
Death of Edward VII and accession of George V
Miners' strike
Budget passed by Lords
Conciliation Bill on women's vote
Parliament Bill passed by Commons and rejected by Lords
Second general election leads to similar result
Opening of Post-Impressionist exhibition in London
1911 Parliament Bill passed
National Insurance Act
Payment of MPs
Strikes by seamen, dockers and railwaymen
Agadir crisis
Churchill becomes First Lord of the Admiralty
1912 Strikes by miners and dockers
Minimum Wages Act for miners
Loss of the *Titanic*
Death of Captain Scott and his party in the Antarctic
'Cat and Mouse' Act
Home Rule Bill introduced
Ulster Covenant to oppose Home Rule signed
First Balkan war
1913 Second Balkan war
Death of suffragette, Emily Davison, at the Derby
Formation of Ulster Volunteer Force
1914 Curragh Mutiny
Triple alliance of miners, rail and transport workers
Formation of Irish Volunteer Force
Assassination of Austrian Archduke at Sarajevo
Home Rule Bill passed but suspended
Britain declares war on Germany

1 MEETING THE EDWARDIANS

The sinking of the *Titanic* on her maiden voyage in 1912 made some of the biggest headlines in the Edwardian popular press. This great liner, the largest ship in the world, had been built in Belfast to new standards of comfort and luxury and equipped with the latest Marconi wireless telegraphy apparatus. She set off for New York on 10 April with about 2200 people on board; the passengers included globe-trotting millionaires seeking pleasure, English and American businessmen seeking trade, and emigrants (from England, Ireland and Europe) seeking a new life. On 14 April the *Titanic* hit an iceberg in the Atlantic and during the two hours she took to sink about 700 escaped in the twenty lifeboats provided. These survivors were picked up by the liner *Carpathia*, which had responded to distress calls over the radio.

The loss of the liner, and the circumstances in which it occurred, caused much comment and controversy. Some crew members had such faith that British technology had created an 'unsinkable' ship that they launched half-empty lifeboats. Others enforced the rule of 'women and children first' at gunpoint. However, proportionately more first-class passengers, whose promenade deck contained the lifeboats, were saved than second- or third-class passengers. In short, the whole story suggests a materialistic, itinerant, complacent, gallant and hierarchical society - which might be regarded as a fair indication of what Edwardian Britain was like [A-B].

The *Titanic's* emigrant passengers were among a record 468,000 who left Britain in 1912. This accelerating trend encouraged anxieties about the size and quality of the population. There was not much consolation in the fact that immigration was increasing too. On the contrary, the influx of thousands of Jews escaping persecution in eastern Europe caused so much alarm about impending 'race suicide' that in 1905 a law was passed to limit the immigration of 'aliens'. Edwardians also worried that members of the upper and middle class were not having enough children. As it happened, the population rose steadily (from 41.5 million in 1901 to 45.25 million in 1911) because the death-rate was falling, especially among infants [C-D].

Another form of migration was from the countryside to towns, which contained three-quarters of the population by 1911. Cities sprawled outwards into red-brick suburbs, connected to the centre by new, cheap forms of transport like trams, underground railways and motor-buses. Nevertheless it was more common for Edwardians to live in smaller

7

provincial towns, where they were closer both in space and in habits to the old rural environment, which many still craved. A fashionable idea of the time, propounded by Ebenezer Howard, was to combine the advantages of town and country by planning 'garden' cities or suburbs. Letchworth and Hampstead Garden Suburb were built along these lines but they had few imitators. Most towns remained overcrowded and unhealthy, with a higher mortality rate than country areas in spite of the better wages they offered [E-F].

The rigid stratification on board the *Titanic* reflected the shape of British society, which, according to Jose Harris, was 'more unequal than at any other period in national history'. The aristocratic upper class remained very rich, in spite of the declining value of their land and the imposition of death duties on their estates after 1894. Old titled families increasingly invested in industry or commerce, and accepted into their ranks *nouveaux riches* who had made money in these fields. In their country mansions and town houses these leisured families, led by King Edward VII, conspicuously displayed their wealth, whether it was new or old, in lavish meals, fine fashions and expensive new hobbies like golf and motoring [G-H and Chapter 5].

The middle class was also growing. In its upper ranks, successful professional and business men lived well on incomes of about £700 a year (and sometimes much more). They kept servants and had plenty of time for such pursuits as the theatre, musical evenings and entertaining along the lines recommended by Mrs Beeton. Her ever-popular cookery book was also directed at 'ordinary middle-class households' like those of doctors, clergymen or bank managers earning from £300 to £700 a year; for them she recommended suitable dinner party menus, stipulating that they should be 'written in French as well as English'. The lower middle class, consisting of office clerks, elementary school teachers, shop assistants and such like on incomes of less than £3 a week, found it a struggle to keep up genteel appearances. They formed a ready audience for the *Daily Mail*, which began publication in 1896. Alfred Harmsworth knew his customers liked 'to read papers which seem intended for persons of superior social standing' and also that many of them could not afford a penny paper. So, he sold the *Mail* for a halfpenny, attaining a circulation of three-quarters of a million throughout the Edwardian period [I-J].

The poorer white-collar workers (especially female ones) sometimes earned less than skilled craftsmen, who were well paid in comparison with those of other countries and former times. On an average wage of 40 shillings a week, their families sometimes had money to spare for such modern luxuries as a sewing-machine or a bicycle, and leisure for new amusements like the cinema or the football match. But for them and for lower-paid unskilled labourers life was precarious. It only took a common

circumstance like redundancy, illness, the birth of more children, old age
or (less commonly than their social superiors supposed) drunkenness, for
families to fall into real poverty. On an income of less than 18 shillings a
week respectability, comfort, leisure and health were well-nigh impossible;
until the Liberal reforms after 1908 only charity or the help of neighbours
could prevent destitution [K-L and Chapter 4].

Thus, although there was some movement, the old social order
remained intact. Most Edwardians knew their place; they deferred to their
superiors and expected deference from their inferiors. There was change,
however, in the way people felt about class. Because they travelled more,
read the new popular press and saw advertisements for tempting
consumer goods, the poorer classes were more aware of how the rich lived
and of their own relative deprivation. Many wanted to narrow the gap. At
the same time social investigators like Booth and Rowntree, socialist
groups like the Fabians and popular writers like Galsworthy, Arnold
Bennett, G.B. Shaw and H.G. Wells pressed for a radical redistribution of
wealth [M-N].

In their personal lives such authors tended to stand outside the English
class system or to escape it by living abroad. The artists and intellectuals of
the Bloomsbury group, including Lytton Strachey, E.M. Forster, Maynard
Keynes, Leonard and Virginia Woolf, and Clive and Vanessa Bell, flouted
both social and sexual conventions in what Forster called the 'battle
against sameness'. It was said of them that all the couples were triangles
and lived in squares. Their liaisons and style of living have tended to
colour the popular image of the Edwardian age rather more than their
numbers justify. Most Edwardians (like the passengers on the *Titanic*)
followed the code of behaviour expected of their class and sex [O].

A A cartoon in the socialist *Daily Herald*

Fifty-eight "men" of the first-class were saved; one hundred and thirty-four steerage women and
children were lost.

9

B An analysis of the survivors from the official inquiry into the disaster [No third-class passengers were interviewed]

1st Class

Adult Males	57 out of 175,	or 32.57%
Adult Females	140 out of 144,	or 97.22%
Male children	5 All saved	
Female children	1 All saved	
	203 out of 325,	or 62.46%

2nd Class

Adult Males	14 out of 168,	or 8.33%
Adult Females	80 out of 93,	or 86.02%
Male children	11 All saved	
Female children	13 All saved	
	118 out of 285,	or 41.40%

3rd Class

Adult Males	75 out of 462,	or 16.23%
Adult Females	76 out of 165,	or 46.06%
Male children	13 out of 48,	or 27.08%
Female children	14 out of 31,	or 45.16%
	178 out of 706,	or 25.21%

Crew	212 out of 885,	or 23.96%
Total on board saved	711 out of 2,201,	or 32.30%

The disproportion between the numbers of the passengers saved in the first, second, and third classes is due to various causes, among which the difference in the position of their quarters and the fact that many of the third class passengers were foreigners, are perhaps the most important. ... The disproportion was certainly not due to any discrimination by the officers or crew in assisting the passengers to the boats.

From *Report on the Loss of the SS Titanic* (July 1912)

C Conservative MP, Sydney Buxton, supports the Aliens' Bill

The only class of immigrants to which I have any strong objection are Russians and Poles who, unfortunately, are coming into the country in greater numbers year by year. I am quite certain that very few of them add to the strength, the wealth, or the welfare of the nation. I am sure there is no feeling in regard to this matter because [they] happen to be Jews. The question of race does not arise. The objection we have to them is that they are in a totally different state of civilisation from what we desire in this country; that neither in race, religious feeling, language, nor blood are they suitable or advantageous to us.

The Prime Minister, Arthur Balfour, adds
... these persons are a most undesirable element and are not likely to produce healthy children. ... In my view we have the right to keep out everybody who does not add to the industrial, social, and intellectual strength of the community.

From a debate in the House of Commons, 2 May 1905

D A novel by H.G. Wells voices Edwardian fears about infertility
This is ... a story of activity and urgency and sterility ... [which I should have] called *Waste.* I have told of childless Marion, of my childless aunt, of Beatrice wasted and wasteful and futile. What hope is there for a people whose women become fruitless? It is all one spectacle of forces running to waste, of people who use and do not replace, the story of a country hectic with a wasting, aimless fever of trade and money-making and pleasure-seeking.

From H. G. Wells: *Tono-Bungay* (1909)

E A Liberal writer worries about the effect of town life on the quality of the population
The second generation of immigrants [from the countryside] has been reared in the courts and crowded ways of the great metropolis, with cramped physical accessories, hot, fretful life, and long hours of sedentary or unhealthy toil. The problem of the coming years is just the problem of this New Town type; upon their development and action depend the future progress of the Anglo-Saxon Race, and for the next half-century at least the policy of the British Empire in the world.

From C. Masterman (ed.): *The Heart of the Empire, Discussions of Problems of Modern City Life in England* (1902)

F Ebenezer Howard proposes an ideal Town-Country environment
Town and country *must be married,* and out of this joyous union will spring a new hope, a new life, a new civilization ... My proposal is that there should be an earnest attempt made to organize a migratory movement of population from our overcrowded centres to sparsely settled rural districts ... and that the golden opportunity afforded by the fact that the land to be settled upon has but few buildings or works upon it, shall be availed of in the fullest manner, by so laying out a Garden City that, as it grows, the free gifts of Nature - fresh air, sunlight, breathing room and playing room - shall be still retained in all needed abundance, and by so employing the resources of modern science that Art may supplement Nature, and life may become an abiding joy and delight.

From E. Howard: *Garden Cities of Tomorrow* (1902)

G A Liberal economist illustrates the distribution of wealth

BRITISH INCOMES IN 1904

RICH 1,250,000 persons £585,000,000	COMFORTABLE 3,750,000 persons £245,000,000
POOR **38,000,000 PERSONS** **£880,000,000**	

From L. G. Chiozza Money: *Riches and Poverty* (1905)

H A young aristocrat is portrayed in Vita Sackville-West's semi-autobiographical novel

Sebastian was growing up into an exemplary son, and conducted himself precisely in the way that his mother considered suitable for a young man of his position. He made friends with all the right young men, he brought them home to Chevron, where they became acquainted with Viola [his sister]; he went to balls in London and danced with all the right debutantes, he flirted with all the right young married women; he organised parties on his own behalf, both at Chevron and elsewhere - was it not he who chartered a liner and spent a turbulent weekend with forty friends, steaming up and down the river from London to Gravesend and from Gravesend to London, while the strains of his orchestra floated out to the astonished crowds upon the banks? - he bought the fastest motor on the market and drove it himself, he squandered money, he was picturesque, extravagant, wild.

From V. Sackville-West: *The Edwardians* (1930)

I In her autobiography Vera Brittain describes her middle-class childhood

Not only in its name, Glen Bank, and its white-painted semi-detachment, but in its hunting pictures and Marcus Stone engravings, its plush curtains, its mahogany furniture and its scarcity of books, our house represented all that was essentially middle-class in that Edwardian decade. ... These families were typical of the kind that still inhabit small country towns; the wives 'kept house', and the husbands occupied themselves as branch bank-managers, cautious and unenterprising solicitors, modest business men who preferred caution to experiment, and 'family' doctors whose bedside manner camouflaged their diagnostic uncertainties. Schoolmasters were not encouraged, as my father found their conversation tedious. ... When I became, in 1912, a provincial debutante, decked out in London-bought garments that I did not know how to wear, the War was still two years away and my hospital service more than three. ... I went to dances, paid calls, skated and tobogganed, played a good deal of Bridge and a great deal of tennis and golf, had music lessons and acted in amateur theatricals; in fact I passed my days in all those conventional pursuits with which the leisured young woman of every generation has endeavoured to fill the time that she is not qualified to use.

From V. Brittain: *Testament of Youth* (1933)

J An extract from H.G. Wells' social comedy *Kipps*
[A draper's assistant has unexpectedly come into some money but does not know how he should behave in higher social circles]
He remembered that he was hungry. ... He drifted [along the Strand] to a neat window with champagne bottles, a dish of asparagus and a framed menu of a two-shilling lunch. He was about to enter, when fortunately he perceived two waiters looking at him over the back screen of the window with a most ironical expression, and he sheered off at once. ... There was a wonderful smell of hot food halfway down Fleet Street, and a nice-looking tavern with several doors, but he could not decide which door. His nerve was going under the strain. ... Kipps was getting demoralized, and each house of refreshment seemed to promise still more obstacles to food. He didn't know how you went in, and what was the correct thing to do with your hat; he didn't know what you said to the waiter, or what you called different things; he was convinced absolutely he would fumble ... and look like a fool. Somebody might laugh at him! ... Presently he had drifted into a part of London where there did not seem to be any refreshment places at all.

'Oh, desh!' said Kipps, in a sort of agony of indecisiveness. 'The very nex' place I see, in I go.'

The next place was a fried-fish shop in a little side street, where there were also sausages on a gas-lit grill. He would have gone in, but suddenly a new scruple came to him, that he was too well dressed for the company he could see dimly through the steam sitting at the counter and eating with a sort of nonchalant speed.

From H. G. Wells: *Kipps* (1905)

K Gwen Davies, daughter of a skilled tinworker, recalls her childhood in Port Talbot
[My father] wasn't a very strong man. I can remember mother would go down at eleven o'clock to the works with a drop of lovely Welsh leek soup. I'm afraid she spoilt only the men, and the boys, my

brothers. They seemed to be more pampered than the girls. My mother was a great believer in good manners, organisation, method. ... When she'd cook everything was back as she was using it, there was no mess on the tables. I never saw such a tidy person. ... She would read the paper from beginning to end, and take it in like blotting paper. ... She wasn't very keen on us having punishment. She liked awakening our conscience. ... We had a very happy home, full of life. On Sundays the whole brood of seven marched down from the [Methodist] church dressed immaculately. She had a great pride in dressing herself and the family. ... We'd no time to breathe, we were so occupied in our church. [At Christmas there was] a big tea, tarts, trifles, everything else and, all the crowd, the house was always packed. And then there was music in the front room, singing hymns, carols - it was quite a day. [Sometimes] families would go to the beach. We'd have a whale of a time. With baskets full of food ... and they used to make what they called herb beer. ... There would be a fire lit and we'd undress before the fire and go into the sea. ... And the mothers weren't as posh as they are now, all of them wouldn't have bathing costumes, they'd go in their nightdresses, and they would be floating in the sea you know, like a parachute.

From an interview in P. Thompson: *The Edwardians* (1975)

L An extract from a contemporary social investigation into working-class lives

Mr. S., scene-shifter. Wage 24s. Allows wife 22s. Six children alive.

October 19.	s	d
Rent	5	0
Burial insurance	2	0
3/4 cwt of coal	1	0
Wood	0	2
Gas	0	8
Soap, soda	0	4
Bus fares	1	0
Newspaper	0	2
Children's Band of Hope [Sunday School]	0	6
Mending boots	0	6
Material for dress	0	4
Cotton and tape	0	3
	11	11

Left for food 10s 1d

In this family there is no regular provision for clothes, which are paid for as they must be bought. No extra money is at any time forthcoming. Mr. S. clothes himself, but extracts from his wife his newspaper as well as his fares. ... The mother is an excellent needlewoman. ... She is also a wonderful manager, and her two rooms are as clean as

a new pin. This has not prevented her from losing five children. ...
She soon after lost a sixth. The rent is far too low for healthy rooms.

From M. Pember Reeves: *Round About a Pound a Week* (1913)

M An extract from Galsworthy's play *The Silver Box*
[An unemployed worker expresses the resentment which has led him to steal from his wife's employer]
JONES: I see this Barthwick o' yours every day goin' down to Pawlyment snug and comfortable to talk his silly soul out; an' I see that young calf, his son, swellin' it about, and goin' on the razzle-dazzle. Wot 'ave they done that makes 'em any better than wot I am? They never did a day's work in their lives.

From J. Galsworthy: *The Silver Box* (1906)

N An extract from Gita Sowerby's play *Rutherford and Son*
[A daughter explains to her father (a self-made business man) the frustrations which have led her to disgrace him by falling in love with the foreman of his glassworks]
RUTHERFORD: I brought you up for a lady as idle as you please - you might ha' sat wi' your hands afore you from morn till night if ye'd a mind to.
JANET: Me a lady? What do ladies think about, sitting the day long with their hands before them? What have they in their idle hearts?
RUTHERFORD: What more did you want, in God's name?
JANET: Oh, what more! The women down there know what I wanted...with their bairns in their shawls and their men to come home at night time. I've envied them - envied them their pain, their poorness - the very times they hadn't bread. Theirs isn't the dead empty house, the blank o' the moors; they got something to fight, something to be feared of. They got life, those women we send cans o' soup to out o' pity when their bairns are born. Me a lady! with work for a man in my hands, passion for a man in my heart! I'm common - common!
RUTHERFORD: It's a lie! I've risen up. You can't go back on it - my children can't go back.

From G. Sowerby: *Rutherford and Son* (1912)

O Leonard Woolf describes the atmosphere in Bloomsbury in 1911
What was so new and exhilarating to me in the Gordon Square [in the Bloomsbury district of London] of July, 1911 was the sense of intimacy and complete freedom of thought and speech, much wider than in the Cambridge of seven years ago, and above all including women. ... We found ourselves, as young men at Cambridge, taking part in ... a conscious revolt against the social, political, religious,

moral, intellectual, and artistic institutions, beliefs, and standards of our fathers and grandfathers. ... [But] to have discussed some subjects or to have called a (sexual) spade a spade in the presence of Miss Strachey or Miss Stephen would seven years before have been unimaginable; here for the first time I found a much more intimate (and wider) circle in which complete freedom of thought and speech was now extended to Vanessa and Virginia [the Stephen sisters], Pippa and Marjorie [the Strachey sisters].

From L. Woolf: *Beginning Again* (1968)

Questions

1 To what extent is the cartoon (Source A) borne out by the figures revealed in Source B? **(6 marks)**

2 How do Sources C-F illustrate Edwardian concerns about the population? **(6 marks)**

3 How useful is Chiozza Money's analysis of wealth distribution (Source G)? **(4 marks)**

4 Compare the effectiveness of the different types of writing contained in Sources H-L in conjuring up Edwardian people and their attitudes. **(8 marks)**

5 How do Sources M-O question Edwardian social conventions? **(6 marks)**

2 EXPLOITING THE EMPIRE

One of the great heroes of Edwardian Britain was Captain Robert Scott, the Antarctic explorer. His final endeavour was to become the first man to reach the South Pole. When he got there in January 1912 he was bitterly disappointed to find that the Norwegian explorer Roald Amundsen had beaten him to it. Scott and his four companions built a cairn for 'the poor slighted Union Jack' and set off 'for the run home and a desperate struggle', during which they died in agonising circumstances. On the last day Scott wrote in his journal: 'I do not regret this journey which has shown that Englishmen can endure hardships, help one another and meet death with as much fortitude as ever in the past'. His final words were: 'For God's sake look after our people'. Scott's anxiety about his country, his patriotic pride and his dismay at being beaten were shared by many of his contemporaries as they contemplated the state of Britain's economy and Empire.

Once hailed as 'the workshop of the world', Britain had been overtaken not by one other nation but by two. In 1900 both Germany and the USA were producing more industrial goods than it was and in some fields they commanded a greater share of world trade. The challenge was keenest in the newer industries, like electrical and chemical engineering, and in mass-produced goods. Even the home market was invaded. The London underground was electrified largely by American enterprise, the khaki dye for British army uniforms came from Germany and British homes were full of cheap American sewing-machines. A flood of articles and pamphlets, with titles like *The American Invaders* or *Made in Germany*, expressed a general fear that Britain was falling behind [A-C].

But Edwardians were proud that Britain was still the greatest trading nation. She had compensated for the loss of North American and European markets by selling more textiles, metals and machines to underdeveloped countries, especially to those in the British Empire. Britain produced most of the world's ships and much of the coal which powered them. Thus her old industries were increasing their exports without having to innovate. Even so, there was a widening trade gap; but it was made good by flourishing 'invisible exports'. These consisted of payments for Britain's sophisticated banking and insurance services and returns on the increasing amount of British capital invested overseas - again chiefly in the Empire. So businesses remained profitable enough not to feel an urgent need to invest in the expensive new machinery and techniques which would have enabled Britain to compete more effectively in the long run. As Eric Hobsbawm writes: 'The Empire was there to provide a cushion in an increasingly hard world' [D].

Indeed, during the decades in which she had slipped to the position of third industrial nation Britain had acquired the largest empire ever known. By 1900 it covered a sixth of the world's surface and encompassed a quarter of the world's population. It was seen not only as an economic asset but also as a means of civilising 'lesser breeds' - the phrase was coined by Rudyard Kipling in his poem which urged imperialists to take up the 'White Man's Burden'. Edwardians prized their heritage and took part enthusiastically in patriotic events like Empire Day celebrations and imperial exhibitions. But the Boer War of 1899-1902 had shaken their confidence. It had cost over £200 million and more than 20,000 lives - merely to defeat 60,000 rebellious Boers in South Africa. Was Britain still great? Would her splendour be eclipsed by Germany and the USA? Might she even fall victim to the Far Eastern 'yellow peril'? Questions like these haunted Edwardians [E-H].

While some radicals and socialists like L.T. Hobhouse attacked the Empire as 'a hard assertion of racial supremacy and material force', most Liberal and Conservative politicians sought ways of preserving it. However, Conservatives were more aggressive imperialists. They opposed the Liberals' conciliatory measures: the granting of self-government to the Boers in 1906 (without safeguards for non-white South Africans); and the Morley-Minto reforms of 1909 which aimed to appease nationalist Indians by giving them representation on provincial councils [I-K].

The most controversial proposal for solving Britain's economic and imperial problems was tariff reform. The powerful Conservative Colonial Secretary, Joseph Chamberlain, outlined the scheme in May 1903. Britain should protect her farmers and industrialists by imposing tariffs on foreign imports, including food; she should then give preference, in the form of lower duties, to goods from imperial countries, which should all reciprocate. In a series of speeches, Chamberlain expounded the benefits which would ensue: a stronger and more united empire, flourishing businesses, falling unemployment and welfare measures such as old age pensions financed by the new duties [L].

Tariff reform immediately became the hottest political debate of the day. Chamberlain resigned from the Cabinet so that he could support the idea freely; three other ministers resigned because they opposed it utterly; and the young Conservative backbencher, Winston Churchill, crossed the floor of the House for the same reason. For the next three years Chamberlain's Tariff Reform League, backed by growing numbers of Conservative MPs, many businessmen and most daily newspapers (including the vociferous *Daily Express*), waged a propaganda campaign similar to that of the Anti-Corn Law League in the nineteenth century [O].

On the other side were ranged Conservative free traders, the Liberals (for whom free trade was the ideal issue to unite a party split over the Boer War), the fledgling Labour Party and most of the trade unions. Their strongest argument was that tariffs would mean higher prices. But they also claimed that protection would harm British industry because it would encourage domestic inefficiency and international tariff wars [M, N and P].

The decisive Liberal victory of 1906 shows that the tariff reformers had not managed to persuade most British people to abandon free trade. Why should they pay more for food or restrict their markets while there was general prosperity and the Empire was intact? Such sacrifices did not yet seem necessary. Joseph Chamberlain, on the other hand, suffered for his devotion to the cause; he had an incapacitating stroke later in the year and retired from the fray. The Conservative Party too paid a price. Although tariff reform gained increasing support among its MPs, they did not all mean the same thing by it. Some were 'whole hoggers'; some abhorred the social welfare part of the scheme; and some (like their indecisive leader, Arthur Balfour) tended to support protective duties but not imperial preference. These divisions probably contributed to their failure to win the two elections of 1910. Afterwards Balfour and his successor, Bonar Law, vacillated and compromised further on the issue until in 1913 Joseph's son and successor, Austen Chamberlain, announced: 'We are beaten and the cause for which father sacrificed more than life itself is abandoned.'

It seems in retrospect that the signs of weakness in early twentieth-century Britain were the beginning of a decline which was to be accelerated by the First World War. Only a radical reconstruction of industry might have prevented this and it is unlikely that tariff reform would have brought this about. Since it might well have upset the finely-balanced system of international payments which helped to sustain Britain's trade at that time, tariff reform could well have harmed rather than helped the economic situation. 'What should England do to be saved?', asked a journalist in 1901. By 1914 there was still no satisfactory answer. Like Scott in the Antarctic, Britain struggled on [Q].

A   The economic performance of Britain and its competitors

Percentage share of world manufacturing production

Year(s)	UK	Germany	USA
1870	31.8	13.2	23.3
1881-5	26.6	13.9	28.6
1896-1900	19.5	16.6	30.1
1913	14.0	15.7	35.8

From the League of Nations: *Industrialization and World Trade* (1945)

B A journalist sounds a warning note

If the British Empire, with a white population smaller than that of any of the other three leading powers in the world [USA, Germany and Russia], increasing far more slowly and in diminishing ratio, is to maintain its lead or even a second or third place, the average efficiency of its units must be not lower but higher than in other countries, and its Government not less but more vigorous and alert than theirs. Unless the empire is re-engined ... we shall be outstripped. Nothing can avert that result but a renaissance of the whole spirit of the race. [He goes on to deplore] ... the slime of the music-hall song [and] the wild exultation of a huge crowd round a football match. ... The average Briton thinks far more of his sport than of his job, and thinks far too much of sport while at his job.

From Calchas: *Will England Last the Century?* (1901)

C Another journalist argues that it is too late for regeneration

England has grown old, her national virility is exhausted. She has arrived at the stage of senile decay, while the US is just entering upon that of vigorous puberty. ... Her game is up. [He compares Britain to some recently discovered sea creatures] ... with huge, cavernous mouths, always open, ready to swallow all that comes in their way, [that] keep swimming about to and fro, ever in search of prey, and that sometimes, in the eagerness of the pursuit, get out of their depth and rise to the surface, where ... they swell to enormous dimensions and burst asunder. Let men and Empires that live and thrive by preying on their kind, take the lesson to heart.

From W. J. Corbet: *What Should England do to be Saved?* (1901)

D Percentages of British exports going to the Empire

	1870	1890	1900	1913
Cotton goods	34.7	44.1	45.8	51.7
Woollen goods	14.0	20.8	29.4	33.5
All manufactured textiles	26.6	37.2	39.7	43.9
Pig iron and iron goods	21.7	33.5	36.7	48.2

From W. Scholte: *British Foreign Trade from 1700 to the 1930s* (1952)

E Winston Churchill describes Britain's imperial mission

What enterprise that an enlightened community may attempt is more noble and more profitable than the reclamation from barbarism of fertile regions and large populations? To give peace to warring tribes, to administer justice where all was violence, to strike the chains off the slave, to draw the richness from the soil, to plant the earliest seeds of commerce and learning, to increase in whole peoples their capacities for pleasure and diminish their chance of pain - what more beautiful ideal or more valuable reward can inspire human effort?

From Winston Churchill: *The River War* (1899)

F   Two memories of imperialism as part of the school curriculum
Bill Woods
They used to encourage us to be proud of the flag, salute the flag
when we was at school. Yes, I was proud of being British. We was
always taught to be proud of the Queen and King. We was the people
of the world, wasn't us?
Edna Rich
I loved poetry, and the school was assembled and they stood me on
top of the headmistress's desk, and I had a Union Jack draped around
me. And I had to recite, 'Oh, where are you going to, all you big
steamers? To fetch England's own grain up and down the great sea.
I'm going to fetch your bread and your butter.' And somehow or other
it stirred a bit of rebellion in me. I thought, where's my bread, where's
my butter? And I think it sowed the first seeds of socialism in me, it
really did.

From S. Humphries: *Hooligans or Rebels?* (1981)

G   The poem remembered by Edna Rich was written for a history
**   textbook by Rudyard Kipling**
'Oh, where are you going to, all you Big Steamers,
With England's own coal, up and down the salt seas?'
'We are going to fetch you your bread and your butter,
Your beef, pork, and mutton, eggs, apples, and cheese.'

'And where will you fetch it from, all you Big Steamers,
And where shall I write you when you are away?'
'We fetch it from Melbourne, Quebec, and Vancouver,
Address us at Hobart, Hong-Kong, and Bombay.'

'Then what can I do for you, all you Big Steamers,
Oh what can I do for your comfort and good?'
'Send out your big warships to watch your big waters,
That no one may stop us from bringing you food.

For the bread that you eat and the biscuits you nibble,
The sweets that you suck and the joints that you carve,
They are brought to you daily by all us Big Steamers,
And if anyone stops our coming you'll starve!'

From C. R. L. Fletcher and R. Kipling: *A School History of England* (1911)

H   A left-wing poet takes a very different view
    And this Thing [England] cries for Empire

    This Thing from all her smoky cities and slums, her idiot
clubs and drawing-rooms, and her brokers' dens,
    Cries out to give her blessings to the world!

And even while she cries
Stand Ireland and India at her doors
In rags and famine.

These are her blessings of Empire!
Ireland (dear Sister-Isle, so near at hand, so fertile, once
so prosperous),
Rack-rented, drained, her wealth by absentees in London
wasted, her people with deep curses emigrating;
India the same - her life-blood sucked - but worse:
Perhaps in twenty tears five hundred millions sterling,
from her famished myriads,
Taken to feed the luxury of Britain,
Taken without return -
While Britain wonders with a pious pretence of innocence
Why famine follows the flag.

From E. Carpenter: 'Empire' in *Towards Democracy* (1905)

I   The Liberals' approach to the empire is exemplified by Lord Morley's moderate Indian Councils Bill
In the future the same end [efficient administration] will have to be attained by association, by co-operation, by persuasion in the day-to-day work of government, instead of by direction, instruction, and command. ... If India is to be contented, prosperous, and progressive, first and foremost, British rule must be strong and stable beyond dispute. But if it is to be strong and stable it must be progressive, and it can only be progressive by giving to the Indians something to live for; by associating them freely and generously in the administration and Government of the country.

From a speech in the House of Commons by Mr Buchanan, 1 April 1909

J   A radical MP questions Britain's right to rule India
It gives me great pleasure to congratulate the Secretary of State for India on reversing the Tory policy pursued during the last ten years. I particularly congratulate Lord Morley on introducing an Indian into the Viceroy's Executive. ... It is an acknowledgement of a great and noble principle - that the people of every country have the right to take part in the government of their country. ... But one feels that it is a very tiny and a very modest step. We have been waiting a long time for that. ... We have been discussing for some time in this House the probability or possibility of invasion of this country by Germany and I was astonished to see honourable members opposite paint a terrible picture of the humiliation if we had an invasion and were governed by a German bureaucracy. I sympathise with them; but why cannot we put ourselves, after all, in the position of the Indians and realise the

humiliation and shame and degradation which injures their countrymen when they are ordered about by British officials? It is a patriotic
and proper sentiment that they have to govern their own country.

From a speech in the House of Commons by Dr Rutherford, 1 April 1909

K Most Conservatives disagreed with the Indian Councils Bill on principle

It is absolutely known throughout India that the natives of all classes,
Hindu and Mahomedan alike, prefer that their affairs should be
administered and their disputes settled by an Englishman rather than
by a native judge or a native administrator, however clever. ... They
prefer this because Englishmen are not subject to false ideas and to
pressure which must take place from a man's family or a man's
surroundings when he is a member of the Indian Civil Service. Natives
look upon Englishmen as the very fount of justice and the basis of
impartiality.

From a speech in the House of Commons by Mr Joynson-Hicks, 29 April
1909

L Joseph Chamberlain inaugurates his Tariff Reform campaign

You want an Empire? (Hear, hear.) Do you think it better to cultivate
the trade with your own people or to let that go in order that you
may keep the trade of those who, rightly enough, are your competi-
tors and rivals? ... I say the people of this Empire ... have two
alternatives before them. They may maintain ... the policy [of free
trade] in all its severity, although it is repudiated by every other nation
and by all your own colonies. ... The second alternative is that we
should insist that we will not be bound by any purely technical
definition of free trade, that, while we seek as one chief object free
interchange of trade and commerce between ourselves and all the
nations of the world, we will nevertheless recover our freedom,
resume that power of negotiation, and if necessary, retaliation (loud
cheers), whenever our own interests or our relations between our
colonies and ourselves are threatened by other people. (Cheers.) I
leave the matter in your hands. I desire that a discussion on this
subject should be opened. ... You have an opportunity; you will never
have it again.

From a speech at Birmingham reported in *The Times*, 16 May 1903

M Asquith leads the Liberal counter-attack

You will have raised for an indefinite time the price of bread and
probably of meat, which is a necessary food of our people. ... You will
raise ... the price of the raw material of some of our most important
manufactures. What does that mean? It means that by adding to the
cost of production you will, under the stress of industrial competition,

still further handicap your trade in every neutral market. You will have fostered at home ... the growth of artificially protected industries. ... You will have jealousy, discontent, a clamour as between different interests at home, and as between different members of the Empire, as to their relative share in the preference which, it will be alleged, is being unfairly given to one and unfairly withheld from others. Finally, you will have all round the world a war of tariffs with those foreign countries which are today your best customers.

From a speech at Caxton Hall, Westminster, 1 July 1903

N The Labour Representation Committee claims

WE ARE MORE THAN FREE TRADERS

We do not regard Free Trade as in any way offering a solution to the problem of poverty. It is economically sound, and so we support it at the present crisis. It is right so far as it goes. Free Trade has enabled us to accumulate National Wealth; a Labour Policy must now supplement Free Trade to enable us to distribute that wealth equitably.

From an LRC policy statement, 1906

O A Tariff Reform poster produced for the election of 1906

P A Liberal Party poster produced for the election of 1906

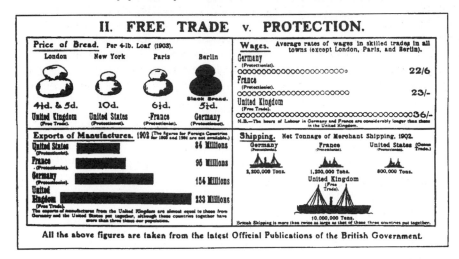

Q A modern historian sums up Britain's position in the world
In the several decades before the First World War Great Britain had
found itself overtaken industrially by both the United States and
Germany, and subjected to intense competition in commercial,
colonial, and maritime spheres. Nonetheless, its combination of
financial resources, productive capacity, imperial possessions, and
naval strength meant that it was still probably the 'number-one' world
power, even if its lead was much less marked than in 1850. Britain
was now a mature state, with a built-in interest in preserving existing
arrangements or, at least, in ensuring that things altered slowly and
peacefully.

From P. Kennedy: *The Rise and Fall of the Great Powers* (1989)

Questions

1 How appropriate are Sources B and C as comments on the statistics in
Source A? **(6 marks)**

2 What can be learnt from Sources D-H about Britain's relationship
with the Empire? **(6 marks)**

3 Compare the attitudes towards Indians in Sources I-K. **(6 marks)**

4 Evaluate the arguments on free trade used in Sources L-P. **(8 marks)**

5 How valid is the comment on Edwardian Britain in Source Q?
(4 marks)

3 IMPROVING THE YOUTH

'There is one beautiful sight in the East End, and only one', wrote Jack London in *The People of the Abyss* when describing his hideous experiences of slum life in 1902. 'It is the children dancing in the street when the organ grinder goes his round. It is fascinating to watch them ... the next generation, swaying and stepping, with pretty little mimicries and graceful inventions all their own, with muscles that move swiftly and easily, and bodies that leap airily, weaving rhythms never taught in dancing school' [A].

Such freedom of expression was unusual for Edwardian children of any class. It is true that the latest child care manuals placed less emphasis on discipline and stressed the importance of fresh air, play and exercise. And popular new children's literature like James Barrie's *Peter Pan* and Kenneth Grahame's *Wind in the Willows* conjured up other worlds of carefree adventure. Nevertheless, the overwhelming impression given in accounts of those who were young at this time is that the regime both at home and at school was exceedingly strict. Rules were generally enforced by the threat of corporal punishment [B-E].

Edwardians were more than usually concerned about the rearing of children. Britain's declining industrial position in the world and the reverses suffered during the Boer War raised fears of national deterioration. In 1901 the social investigator Seebohm Rowntree found that nearly 30 per cent of the population of York were unable to maintain the 'physical efficiency' of their families. In 1902 General J.F. Maurice asserted that 60 per cent of Englishmen were unfit for military service. People (especially middle-class professionals) became preoccupied with the question of how to improve the nation's youth [F].

Various answers were advanced. It was a matter, said Beatrice Webb, of 'raising the standard of the health and conduct of the mass of our race ... in order to hold our own with such highly regulated races as the Germans and the Japanese'. George Bernard Shaw suggested 'selective breeding'. This 'eugenic' solution attracted some support. So did calls for radical social reforms, such as the maintenance grants for mothers proposed by H.G. Wells. Beatrice Webb and her husband Sidney, Shaw and Wells all belonged to a group within the left-wing Fabian Society who called themselves the Co-Efficients. Their natural enemies on the right, meanwhile, demanded conscription or supported character-training schemes like Scouting. But the aims of crusaders for 'national efficiency' were so similar that they often called for multi-party coalitions to deal with the emergency [G-I].

Practising politicians were wary of extreme solutions, especially as the Committee on Physical Deterioration reported in 1904 that, while there were many evils to be remedied, there was no 'progressive racial deterioration'. Conservatives were reluctant to increase government expenditure; Liberals disliked measures which would diminish individual liberty; and the Labour Party rejected the cult of efficiency in favour of improving the quality of life. Nevertheless the widespread alarm helped to inspire reforms which, whatever motive lay behind them, made life better for British children in the long run [J].

The Conservative government's main achievement was the Education Act of 1902. This abolished the outdated School Boards and put local councils in charge of elementary education, including the voluntary denominational schools, which retained some independence in religious matters and in the appointment of teachers. The Co-Efficients applauded the reorganisation because, as Sidney Webb said, it made education a 'public function'. The Liberals opposed it, largely on behalf of Nonconformists who objected to the support of Anglican and Catholic schools out of local rates. The councils also had to control and develop a separate system of secondary education to replace the 'higher-grade' courses which some elementary schools had developed in response to demand. No method of transition from the elementary to the secondary level was laid down until 1907, when scholarships were introduced by which clever children could gain free secondary-school places. By 1914 the number of secondary schools had doubled, but only one in forty elementary-school pupils went on to them. The successful ones were more often boys than girls and more often from the lower middle than from the working class. The vast majority of children still left school at thirteen. Richer parents continued to buy education for their offspring, usually in grammar and public schools [K-L].

Eventually the Liberals had to accept the Education Act. Although their championing of the Nonconformist cause helped them to win the 1906 election, they were unable to pass their proposed amendments through the House of Lords. Denominational schools were here to stay. The Liberals turned their attention to the physical rather than the religious welfare of school pupils. Surveys like Rowntree's had revealed a vast gulf in fitness between children of different classes. Their shocking statistics helped to convince reluctant MPs that the state must intervene to help children who were too hungry or too unhealthy to derive much benefit from any system of schooling. After 1907 local education authorities could provide mid-day meals and clinics in schools. Progress was slow but by 1914 nearly half the councils were feeding pupils and about three quarters were giving them some medical treatment. The rights and needs of children were further spelt out in the Children's

Charter of 1908. In spite of all these efforts (as well as those of private charities and missions), an inquiry of 1913 could still point to the 'underfed school child' as 'a disgrace and a danger to the State'. Conservatives, on the other hand, condemned these reforms for sapping self-reliance and creating what modern right-wingers call 'the nanny-state' [M-P].

A great champion of self-reliance was General Robert Baden-Powell, who founded the popular Boy Scout movement in 1908. Some contemporaries criticised it, as historians have done since, as a militaristic 'character-factory' designed to forge soldiers for the nation. But a recent biography sees Scouting as 'a blessed escape from national and personal self-doubt'. Many lads (and their leaders) found security in wholesome, adventurous pursuits like camping and tracking. Most of them were middle-class (as were the Girl Guides, founded in 1910) even though Baden-Powell tried hard to attract slum children and 'street corner loafers'. But the uniform was too expensive. Also older working-class boys and girls were usually too busy earning extra pennies for the family kitty or helping with the household chores to prolong their childhood in this organised fashion [Q-R].

In the twelve years following Jack London's descent into the abyss much thought and effort were devoted to improving Britain's youth. It was too short a time for real progress to be apparent. On the eve of the First World War, conditions in the East End and other poverty-stricken places were still appalling. As Maud Pember Reeves said, 'want of joy was the most salient feature of the children as they grew older'. But when the organ-grinder came they still, no doubt, danced.

A London girls dancing to a street organ, 1902

28

B A child care manual gives the latest advice on play

Provide the child with Nature's gifts - earth (sand or clay for mud pies, gardening), water (bubble-blowing, boat-sailing, canal-making), fire (bonfire, poker-work), air (whistles, air-bladders, air-balloons, kites, aeroplanes, windmills), and give him wood, paper, calico, string, glue, hammer and nails, and any other necessary materials, and you are giving him things that are worth to him thousands of ready-made toys. ... Outdoor play whenever weather permits it is most desirable; failing that, a large upper room or attic should be set aside, where children can romp or rampage, where there are no knick-knacks to be broken, the chairs are plain and strong, convertible into trains, the inverted table into a boat. ... For outdoor play, let us hope the garden is sufficiently roomy, admitting of games such as hide-and-seek, I spy, tag, rounders, croquet, tennis, and acting historical scenes such as sighting the Armada, Sir Philip Sidney at the Battle of Zutphen, the landing of the Pilgrim Fathers, the discovery of the North Pole, and boy scouting.

From Amy Barnard: *The Home Training of Children* (1910)

C Wendy enjoys her new life in Neverland

As time wore on did she think much about the beloved parents she had left behind her? ... I am afraid that Wendy did not really worry about her father and mother; she was absolutely confident that they would always keep the nursery window open for her to fly back by, and this gave her complete ease of mind. ... Adventures, of course, as we shall see, were a daily occurrence. ... We might tell how Peter saved Tiger Lily's life in the Mermaids' Lagoon, and so made her his ally. ... Quite as exciting was Tinker Bell's attempt, with the help of some street fairies, to have the sleeping Wendy conveyed on a great floating leaf to the mainland. Fortunately the leaf gave way and Wendy woke, thinking it was bath-time, and swam back. Or again, we might choose Peter's defiance of the lions, when he drew a circle round him on the ground with an arrow and defied them to cross it; and though he waited for hours, with the other boys and Wendy looking on breathlessly from the trees, not one of them dared to accept his challenge.

From J.M. Barrie: the book version of *Peter Pan* (1911)

D Less idyllic evocations of childhood
(i) Thomas Morgan, born 1892, a poor London child

We the littlest ones, we were served last. Whatever she [their mother] got we had to have. You couldn't pick and choose. We were never allowed to put our arms on the table, like that. 'Get them arms off!' Wallop - you know. Put a knife in your mouth - you got a hiding for that. Oh, she taught us good manners as far as she could go.

(ii) Clifford Hills, born 1904, a poor country child
Mother used a stick sometimes, a little cane, but not violently, we had
to be corrected. ... But my parents weren't cruel at all, they used to
correct us properly. They were kind and good to us and they used no
bad language. ... And we were taught, of course, never to be rude to
people or to answer back.

(iii) Esther Stokes, born 1895, a wealthy middle-class child
The discipline was pretty terrific really. I mean, take tea-time, always
bread and butter first you know. Never any jam or anything till you'd
had your bread and butter. Aggie [the nurse] would watch everything.
The discipline in the nursery was tremendous.

(iv) Joan Poynder, born 1897, an upper-class child
I remember being punished, I think rather unfairly too, for quite small
things really. I mean grown ups were irritated. I don't know why, not
being obedient or something. ... You might be sent to bed or you
were scolded.

From interviews in Thea Thompson: *Edwardian Childhoods* (1981)

E   The daughter of a writer recalls a lonely childhood
Not until [my brother] Henry and I were in our teens did we meet
visitors, many of whom never knew that our parents had children, so
we grew up morbidly shy and undemonstrative. With our naturally
introspective natures and hidden lives of the imagination, we spent
most of our early lives in private worlds, remote from the grown-ups.
But this secretiveness ran through the household. Father had his work,
Mother her social life of tea-parties and paying calls, both with
numerous admirers and lovers. Nanny had her mother and siblings in
whom our parents took no interest, or in the servants and their
outside affairs and families. Even Gaffer the cat went his own
independent way and Nanny's fox terrier, Flip, was not allowed into
the garden. ... [When sent to boarding school] Henry became a target
for school bullies; yet our parents were still determined that he should
conform to the narrow standards of Edwardian middle-class society,
education and morality, against which I had begun forcibly to rebel.

From Adelaide Ross: *Reverie* (1981)

F   An imperialist writer laments the state of the youth
A vast population has been created by the factory and industrial
systems, the majority of which is incapable of bearing arms. Specta-
cled school-children hungry, strumous [with swollen glands], and
epileptic, grow into consumptive bridegrooms and scrofulous brides,
and are assured beforehand of the blessing of the Church, the aid of
the compassionate, and such solace as hospitals provided wholesale
by unknown donors can supply. If a voice be raised in protest against
the unhealthy perversion of the command, 'Be ye fruitful and multiply'

it is drowned in a chorus of sickly emotion.

From A. White: *Efficiency and Empire* (1901)

G Shaw's eugenic solution
What is proposed is nothing but the replacement of the old unintelli-
gent, inevitable, almost unconscious fertility by an intelligently
controlled, conscious fertility, and the elimination of the mere
voluptuary [sensual person] from the evolutionary process. ... In short,
the individual instinct in this matter, overwhelming as it is thought-
lessly supposed to be, is really a finally negligible one. ... We must
replace the man by the superman. ... We must eliminate the Yahoo
[brute], or his vote will wreck the commonwealth.

From G.B. Shaw: *Man and Superman* (1903)

H H.G. Wells sees the State as the Over-Parent
People rear children for the State and for the future; if they do that
well they do the world a service, and deserve payment. ... It follows
that motherhood ... is regarded by the Socialists as a benefit to
society, a public duty done. ... The State will pay for children born
legitimately in the marriage it will sanction. A woman with healthy
and successful offspring will draw a wage for each one of them from
the State, so long as they go on well. It will be her wage. Under the
State she will control her child's upbringing. ... So, the monstrous
absurdity of women discharging their supreme social function, bearing
and rearing children in their spare time, as it were, while they 'earn
their living' by contributing to some trivial industrial product, will
disappear.

From an article in *Independent Review* (1906)

**I A school textbook explains what England needs to defend itself
against its rivals**
I don't think there can be any doubt that the only safe thing for all of
us who love our country is to learn soldiering at once, and to be
prepared to fight at any moment. [After describing England's material
progress it concludes] In the common sense of the word 'happy',
these and a thousand other inventions have no doubt made us
happier than our great-grandfathers were. Have they made us better,
braver, more self-denying, more manly men and boys, more tender,
more affectionate, more home-loving women and girls? It is for you
boys and girls, who are growing up, to resolve that you will be all
these things, and to be true to your resolutions.

From Fletcher and Kipling: *A School History of England* (1911)

J The Physical Deterioration Committee takes an optimistic view
There appears to be very little real evidence on the pre-natal side to

account for the widespread physical degeneracy among the poorer population. There is, accordingly, every reason to anticipate RAPID amelioration of physique so soon as improvement occurs in external conditions, particularly as regards food, clothing, overcrowding, cleanliness, drunkenness, and the spread of common practical knowledge of home management. In fact, all evidence points to *active, rapid improvement, bodily and mental, in the worst districts,* so soon as they are exposed to better circumstances, even the weaker children recovering at a later stage from the evil effects of infant life.

[Among the Committee's recommendations are] public nurseries ... instruction in schools on the laws of health, including the demonstr-ation of the physical evils caused by drinking ... the systematic instruction in continuation classes of girls in the processes of infant feeding and management ... medical inspection of children at school ... provision by the Local Authorities for dealing with the question of underfed children ... compulsory drill and physical exercises [for boys] ... prohibition of the sale of tobacco and cigarettes to children.

From the Committee *Report* (1904)

K A Liberal economist points out the deficiencies of the education system after 1902

Education is the opportunity of opportunities. ... But the battle in this country is far from won. For consider what equal opportunity of knowledge and culture implies. It implies that neither poverty, nor ignorance of parents, nor premature wage-earning, nor defects of teaching apparatus, shall keep any person from any sort of learning which will improve his understanding, elevate his character, and increase his efficiency as a worker and a citizen. Now we have hardly begun to realise these essentials in our system of education, where not five per cent of the working classes get anything beyond the barest rudiments. ... What is needed is not an educational ladder ... to be climbed with difficulty by a chosen energetic few, who ... are absorbed in official and professional occupations which dissociate them from the common life of the people. It is a broad, easy stair ... that is wanted, one which will entice everyone to rise, will make for general and not for selected culture.

From J. A. Hobson: *The Crisis of Liberalism* (1909)

L Adults recall their experiences of Edwardian education
(i) Clifford Hills, born 1904

I had so many jobs to do before I went to school, so I couldn't help being late sometimes. Clean the knives, clean shoes, sift cinders, clean the dogs' kennels, scrub the bath house, no end of jobs to get in. ... That was when I was kitchen boy and then of course I had the same work to do when I left school, plus going with the farmer in his pony and cart round the farms. ... They expected so much from a boy of nine.

(ii) Annie Wilson, born 1898, a poor Nottingham child

We had to take an examination to see if we were clever enough to go for a scholarship for Huntingdon Street school where they had to pay you see ... Huntingdon Street school had the boys and girls of better class people, business people mostly, and if they'd got one or two vacancies they'd let them in from the board schools ... I shouldn't have been more than ten when I went there. And I stayed there until I was thirteen and could leave. ... When you left school at thirteen you got any job you could get because you was going to take five shillings home and it was gold to you.

(iii) Florence Atherton, born 1890, a lower middle-class child

The teachers seemed to do a lot for us after school hours. Always something going on, socials, dances, teaching us, going to school after school hours and showing us how to do things. ... I liked going to school very much but I didn't learn enough. I always wanted to learn more. But we were too poor to be sent anywhere else. I was always quick at a lot of things. I never missed a class. But I always remember that those whose parents were teachers ... always won the scholarship. If they got a scholarship they went to Mount St. Joseph's. ... Well I longed to go but my mother and father were too poor. ... When I left school we had to go to work and some of the girls that had won scholarships and got on and had a good education they'd broke away from us. ... I've always wanted to go to a nice school and wear a uniform. It's strange that, isn't it?

(iv) Geoffrey Brady, born 1898, a middle-class child whose father's business collapsed when he was ten

It was put to me that I might not be able to stay on even at the grammar school. ... My one chance was that I might get a scholarship. ... I worked very hard and I was given the one annual scholarship which was awarded to the hardest working boy in the school. ... At the age of fourteen through some friends I was offered the entry into a very wealthy and very good class firm of flour merchants in Manchester. Well I wasn't given much option about it. My ambition ... was to struggle along and get a scholarship to Oxford or Cambridge. ... But my father came to me, and of course I knew what our financial position was ... and so I left school one Saturday morning and started work on the Monday morning and worked for fifty odd years after that.

From Thea Thompson: *Edwardian Childhoods* (1981)

M Rowntree's statistics reveal the gulf in fitness between different income groups within the working class

Mortality of children under five years of age

Area No. 1 (poorest),   13.96
Area No. 2 (middle),   10.50 ⎫ Per annum per 1000 of all ages living
Area No. 3 (highest),   6.00 ⎬
Whole of York   7.37 ⎭

Average heights at 13 (in inches)

	Boys	Girls
Poorest	55.00	56.25
Middle	56.00	57.50
Highest	58.50	58.00

Average weights at 13 (in pounds)

	Boys	Girls
Poorest	73.00	79.25
Middle	80.00	84.50
Highest	84.25	88.25

From S. Rowntree: *Poverty: A Study of Town Life* (1901)

N Bradford Local Education Authority provides dinners for two pence
Monday: Lentil and tomato soup. Currant roly-poly pudding.
Tuesday: Meat pudding. Ground-rice pudding.
Wednesday: Yorkshire pudding, gravy, peas. Rice and sultanas.
Thursday: Scotch barley broth. Currant pastry or fruit tart.
Friday: Stewed fish, parsley sauce, peas, mashed potatoes. Cornflour blancmange. All these meals included bread.

From *Report of the Working of the Provision of Meals Act* (1909)

O Results of the new medical examinations
Of the children examined approximately one-half of the girls in urban areas, and one-quarter of those in rural areas, have verminous heads. Ringworm has been found to be more widespread than was supposed. It is commonly found that from twenty to forty per cent of all school-children examined, have four or more decayed teeth. Enlargement of the tonsils associated with adenoid growths at the back of the nose is a very prevalent condition. In regard to the children examined who were about to leave school, approximately ten per cent were in need of treatment for visual defect. Ear disease occurring in childhood is a comparatively frequent complaint, and one which is especially likely to follow some of the infectious diseases, particularly scarlet fever. Defective hearing of a degree noticed by the teachers exists in approximately five per cent of school-children.

From *Report of the Chief Medical Officer for the Board of Education* (1908)

P   A Conservative MP opposes the provision of school meals
The effect of this Bill would be to create a body of workingmen who, instead of helping their fellows and standing alone, would be sponging upon their fellow workers. What would be the effect on the child? [An Hon. Member: 'It would be better fed.'] ... If they were to give meals they must also give boots and clothing. Then they must begin to ask under what conditions the child lived, what kind of rooms it slept in, was it washed before it went to bed, and did it sleep in a decent cot at night. ['Hear, hear' from the Labour benches, and cries of 'Why not?'] ... It was not by such methods as these that they would raise the mass of the people to a better condition. In the long run they could only raise people by teaching them to raise themselves, but the effect of this Bill would be to encourage people to degrade themselves.

From a speech by Harold Cox reported in *Hansard*, 2 March 1906

Q   Baden-Powell's Scout Law
3   A SCOUT'S DUTY IS TO BE USEFUL AND TO HELP OTHERS. And he is to do his duty before anything else, even though he gives up his own pleasure, or comfort, or safety to do it. ... And he must try his best to do a good turn to somebody every day.
4   A SCOUT IS A FRIEND TO ALL, AND A BROTHER TO EVERY OTHER SCOUT, NO MATTER TO WHAT SOCIAL CLASS THE OTHER BELONGS. A Scout must never be a SNOB. ... A Scout accepts the other man as he finds him, and makes the best of him.
7   A SCOUT OBEYS ORDERS of his parents, patrol leader, or Scoutmaster without question. Even if he gets an order he does not like ... he must carry it out all the same because it is his duty.
8   A SCOUT SMILES AND WHISTLES under all circumstances.
9   A SCOUT IS THRIFTY, that is he saves every penny he can, and puts it in the bank, so that he may have money when he is out of work, and thus not make himself a burden to others.

From R.S. Baden-Powell: *Scouting for Boys* (1909 edn)

R   A child from Maud Pember Reeves's Lambeth survey
Emma, aged ten, stood about 4 feet 6 inches in her socks. ... She was a queer little figure, the eldest of six, with a baby always in her arms out of school-hours. She was not highly intelligent, but she had a soothing way with children. ... She was sturdy and tough to all appearance, and could scrub a floor or wring out a tubful of clothes in a masterly way. She had a dog-like devotion for a half deaf, half blind little mother, who nevertheless managed to keep two rooms, a husband, and six children in a state of extraordinary order, considering all things. ... Emma's mother found her a great comfort, and very reluctantly sent her to work in a factory at the age of fifteen. There

she earned 6s. a week, and became the family bread-winner during the frequent illnesses of her father.

From M. Pember Reeves: *Round About a Pound a Week* (1913)

Questions

1 In the light of Sources A-E discuss the view that the Edwardian era was a 'golden age' for children. **(7 marks)**

2 Compare the suggestions for improving 'national efficiency' made in Sources F, G, H, I and J, and assess their practicality. **(7 marks)**

3 How useful are Sources K and L in illustrating the opportunities for secondary education after the 1902 Act? **(6 marks)**

4 How valid, in the light of sources M-O, are the objections made in Source P to the Liberal reforms concerning children? **(6 marks)**

5 In what ways might the child in Source R be said to live up to the ideals contained in Source Q? **(4 marks)**

4 TACKLING POVERTY

'We are not concerned with the very poor', wrote E. M. Forster in *Howard's End* (1910). 'They are unthinkable, and only to be approached by the statistician or the poet.' It is indeed rare to find Edwardian novels dealing with poor people. One notable exception is *The Ragged Trousered Philanthropists,* a semi-autobiographical novel by house-painter Robert Tressell, which was rejected by several publishers before being published in 1914 - four years after its author's death from tuberculosis. Questioned in 1994 about literature which had influenced them, Labour MPs cited this powerful indictment of exploitation more than any other book. But what inspired early twentieth-century politicians to develop a new concern for the 'very poor'? [A].

One influence on MPs of all parties was undoubtedly the work done by statisticians. Charles Booth was a pioneer, finding in 1889 that 30 per cent of Londoners were very poor. He was followed by Seebohm Rowntree who revealed in 1901 that 27 per cent of York's population lived below the 'poverty line'. Some of those who dwelt below this line suffered from what he called 'primary poverty': their total family earnings were simply not enough for them to buy the bare essentials. The rest existed in 'secondary poverty': their lives were equally wretched but as a result of expenditure 'either useful or wasteful'. Radical writers like Hobhouse and Hobson urged politicians to adopt programmes of state intervention to tackle poverty - or at least to alleviate that of 'respectable' and 'deserving' families [B and D].

There was little government action before 1906 since the Conservatives were reluctant to spend money in the aftermath of the costly Boer War. But the obvious distress and discontent caused by soaring unemployment led them to pass the Unemployed Workmen's Act of 1905, which gave distress committees limited funds with which to organise relief works. In the same year, Balfour appointed a Royal Commission to inquire into the patently inadequate Poor Law, which was still operating on the old system of providing help for the able-bodied only in workhouses [C].

Between 1906 and 1914 the Liberal government passed an unprecedented number of measures to help the poor. Historians agree that the government was not inspired solely by humanitarian concerns. Ministers wanted to create a more efficient workforce which could rival that of competitor nations, some of whom had already developed welfare schemes. Liberals were also determined to provide their own alternative both to the Conservative idea of social reform financed by tariffs and to the Labour movement's programme of full employment, a minimum wage and generous state benefits. In some cases active pressure groups pushed the government towards particular measures, such as old age pensions, though in general working-class families were suspicious of intrusive welfare schemes. As usual politicians acted from a variety of motives [E-F].

The basic aim of Liberal legislation was to remove from dependence on the Poor Law those whose poverty was not their own fault (children, the old, the sick and the unemployed), while retaining the threat of the workhouse for the idle and the spendthrift. Early measures provided cautious help for needy schoolchildren [Chapter 3]. After 1908 Lloyd George, assisted by Winston Churchill and encouraged by Asquith, was able to speed up his 'ambulance wagon to the relief of the distressed'. How effective was this new effort to help the poor?

About half a million of the poorest seventy year-olds (a majority of whom were women) received pensions of up to five shillings a week - but many old people still had to resort to the workhouse. The National Health Insurance Act of 1911 required manual workers to pay weekly contributions (topped up by employers and by the state), in return for which they received medical treatment as well as sickness and maternity benefits of seven shillings a week. The wives and children of employees were not included and neither were the large numbers of casual or seasonal workers. A similar scheme provided unemployment pay for workmen in the shipbuilding, engineering and construction industries (about a quarter of the workforce). Another source of help for the unemployed were the new Labour Exchanges which, by 1914, were finding jobs for 3000 workers a day. A Development Commission to provide public works was less successful [G-N].

For poverty due to low wages (its most common cause) Liberals were less inclined to find a remedy. Intervention in this sphere smacked too much of socialism. An exception was made for the grossly exploited and largely female workforce in the notorious 'sweated industries' like dress-making; the Trade Boards Act of 1909 arranged for minimum wages to be fixed in four of these trades. And, after Rowntree's exposure in 1913 of the grinding poverty still endured by rural labourers, Lloyd George was considering reforms which would aid the 'hopeless, underpaid, landless drudge on the soil' [O-Q].

Meanwhile the Royal Commission on the Poor Law had completed its work and submitted both a Majority and a Minority Report. These had more in common than their signatories supposed; both condemned the old Poor Law and recommended new systems of relief, while assuming the continued necessity for punitive policies towards the undeserving poor. Beatrice Webb's Minority Report insisted that the various categories of need must be dealt with by separate local authority committees and advocated greater '*disciplinary* supervision' over people seeking help. In fact the Liberals did not abolish the Poor Law, which survived until 1929. Nevertheless, as a result of their measures the number of paupers in its 'care' fell drastically and the amount of government money spent on the social services more than doubled [R].

The effects as well as the causes of these reforms have been much debated. As far as party politics are concerned, the Gladstonian party of retrenchment and self-help had been transformed into a 'New Liberal' party of redistributive taxation and collective responsibility. But it is difficult to tell whether this change could have ensured its survival as the Conservatives' main adversary or whether the Labour Party was bound to usurp that position [Chapter 10].

And how far-reaching were the reforms? The traditional view is that the Liberals laid the foundations of the post-1945 'welfare state'. More recent historians argue that they devised a limited welfare system in which the poor remained 'guests at the table of an increasingly prosperous society' [S-T].

A Robert Tressell's socialist novel describes the lives of a group of decorators

During the following week the work at 'The Cave' [the house at which they were employed] progressed rapidly towards completion, although the hours of daylight being so few, the men worked only from 8am till 4pm and they had their breakfasts before they came. This made 40 hours a week, so that those who were paid sevenpence an hour earned £1 3s 4d. Those who got sixpence-halfpenny drew £1 1s 8d. Those whose wages were fivepence an hour were paid the princely sum of 16s 8d for their week's hard labour, and those whose rate was fourpence-halfpenny 'picked up' 15s. And yet there are people who have the insolence to say that Drink is the cause of poverty. And many of the persons who say this, spend more money than that on drink themselves - every day of their useless lives. ... The fact that some of Rushton's men spent about two shillings a week on drink when they were in employment was not the cause of their poverty. If they had never spent a farthing for drink, and if their wretched wages had been increased fifty per cent, they would still have been in a condition of the most abject poverty, for nearly all the benefits and privileges of civilisation, nearly everything that makes life worth living, would still have been beyond their reach.

From R. Tressell: *The Ragged Trousered Philanthropists* (1914)

B Rowntree lists the causes of primary poverty in York
Death of chief wage-earner	15.63%
Illness or old age of chief wage-earner	5.11%
Chief wage-earner out of work	2.31%

Irregularity of work	2.83%
Largeness of family, i.e. more than four children	22.16%
In regular work, but at low wages	55.96%

[Rowntree concludes that] *the wages paid for unskilled work in York are insufficient to provide food, shelter, and clothing adequate to maintain a family of moderate size in a state of bare physical efficiency.*

And let us clearly understand what 'merely physical efficiency' means. A family living on the scale allowed for in this estimate must never spend a penny on railway fare or omnibus. They must never go into the country unless they walk. They must never purchase a halfpenny newspaper or spend a penny to buy a ticket for a popular concert. They must write no letters to absent children, for they cannot afford the postage. They must never contribute anything to the church or chapel, or give any help to a neighbour which costs them money. They cannot save, nor can they join sick club or Trade union, because they cannot pay the necessary subscriptions. The children must have no pocket money for dolls, marbles, or sweets. The father must smoke no tobacco, and must drink no beer. The mother must never buy any pretty clothes for herself or for her children. ... If any of these conditions are broken, the extra expenditure involved is met, *and can only be met,* by limiting the diet; or, in other words, by sacrificing physical efficiency. ... That in this land of abounding wealth, during a time of perhaps unexampled prosperity, probably more than one-fourth of the population are living in poverty, is a fact which may well cause great searchings of heart.

From S. Rowntree: *Poverty: A Study of Town Life* (1901)

C Jack London spends a night in the Whitechapel workhouse

At six o'clock we were admitted in groups of three. Name, age, occupation, place of birth, condition of destitution, and the previous night's 'doss', were taken with lightning-like rapidity by the superintendent; and as I turned I was startled by a man's thrusting into my hand something that felt like a brick, and shouting into my ear, 'Any knives, matches, or tobacco?' 'No, sir,' I lied, as lied every man who entered. As I passed downstairs to the cellar, I looked at the brick in my hand, and saw that by doing violence to the language, it might be called 'bread'. ... The light was very dim down in the cellar, and before I knew it some other man had thrust a pannikin into my other hand. Then I stumbled on to a still darker room, where were benches and tables and men. The place smelled vilely. ... The pannikin contained skilly, three-quarters of a pint, a mixture of Indian corn and hot water. The men were dipping their bread into heaps of salt scattered over the dirty tables. I attempted the same, but the bread seemed to stick in my mouth. ... I struggled manfully, but half-a-dozen mouthfuls of

skilly and bread was the measure of my success. ... By seven o'clock
we were called away to bathe and go to bed. ... The sleeping
compartment was a long, narrow room, traversed by two long iron
rails. Between these were stretched pieces of canvas, six feet long and
less than two feet wide. These were the beds, and they were six
inches apart and about eight inches above the floor. ... Morning came,
with a six o'clock breakfast of bread and skilly ... and we were told off
to our various tasks. Some were set to scrubbing and cleaning, others
to picking oakum, and eight of us were convoyed across the street to
the Whitechapel Infirmary, where we were set at scavenger work. This
was the method by which we paid for our skilly and canvas.

From J. London: *The People of the Abyss* (1903)

D   A sociologist defines the task of a Liberal government
We said above that it was the function of the State to secure the
conditions upon which mind and character may develop themselves.
Similarly we may say now that the State is to secure conditions upon
which its citizens are able to win by their own efforts all that is
necessary to a full civic efficiency. It is not for the State to feed,
house, or clothe them. It is for the State to take care that the
economic conditions are such that the normal man who is not
defective in mind or body can by useful labour feed, house, and
clothe himself and his family. The 'right to work' and the right to a
'living wage' are just as valid as the rights of person and property.
That is to say, they are integral conditions of a good social order ...
[The workman] owes the State the duty of industriously working for
himself and his family. ... On the other hand society owes to him the
means of maintaining a civilized standard of life, and this debt is not
adequately discharged by leaving him to secure such wages as he can
in the higgling of the market.

From L.T. Hobhouse: *Liberalism* (1911)

E   Lloyd George explains the need for new Liberal policies
We have a great Labour Party sprung up. Unless we can prove, as I
think we can, that there is no necessity for a separate party in order
to press forward the legitimate claims of labour, then you will find
that the same thing will happen in England that has happened in
Belgium and Germany - that the Liberal Party will be practically wiped
out, and that in its place you will get a more extreme and revolutionary party, which will sail under the colours of Socialism or Independent Labour. ... It rests with the Liberal Administration which we can
see on the horizon to prevent such a state of things from coming
about.

From a speech reported in the *Manchester Guardian*, 7 November 1904

F Winston Churchill proclaims the 'New Liberalism'

The cause of the Liberal Party is the cause of the left-out millions. ...
No man can be a collectivist alone or an individualist alone. He must
be both an individualist and a collectivist. ... Collectively we have an
Army and a Navy and a Civil Service; collectively we have a Post
Office, and a police, and a Government; collectively we light our
streets and supply ourselves with water; collectively we indulge in all
the necessities of communication. But we do not make love collectively, and the ladies do not marry us collectively, and we do not eat
collectively and we do not die collectively, and it is not collectively
that we face the sorrows and hopes, the winnings and losings of this
world of accident and storm. No view of society can be complete
which does not comprise within its scope both collective organisation
and individual incentive. The evergrowing complications of civilisation
create for us new services which have to be undertaken by the State.
... There is a growing feeling, which I entirely share, against allowing
those services to pass into private hands. ... I look forward to the
universal establishment of minimum standards of life and labour, and
their progressive elevation as the increasing energies of production
may merit.

From a speech by Churchill, 11 October 1906

G Conditions for receipt of the old age pension
[these proved unworkable and were removed in 1919]

1 A person shall be disqualified for receiving or continuing to receive
an old age pension
(a) While he is in receipt of any poor relief ...
(b) If, before he becomes entitled to a pension, he has habitually failed
to work according to his ability, opportunity, and need, for the
maintenance or benefit of himself and those legally dependent on
him ...
(c) While he is detained in any asylum within the meaning of the
Lunacy Act, 1890 ...
2 Where a person has been before the passing of this Act, or is after
the passing of this Act, convicted of any offence, and ordered to be
imprisoned ... he shall be disqualified ... while he is detained in
prison ... and for a further period of ten years after the date on which
he is released from prison.

From the Old Age Pensions Act 1908

H The *Daily Express* reports on the first old age pensioners

Old folks hobbling along the streets with their blue booklets tightly
held in their hands were greeted by all the parish with the cheery cry,
'Got your pension?' ... It was a pathetic sight - the stream of old,
worn men and women, some half-blind, some bent with age and

rheumatism, hobbling along with sticks, some led by neighbours, some moving along by themselves a few steps at a time, shaky and fearful but independent to the last. The most pathetic feature of the payments was the death of several old people as they received their pensions. ... Emmanuel Hawthorne, of Spalding, drew his pension and dropped dead when he returned home, it is supposed that the excitement acted on a weak heart. A woman dropped dead from excitement in Sandwich Post Office at 8 o'clock as she was handed her five shillings.

From the *Daily Express*, 1 January 1909

I Lloyd George defends the contributory principle of the National Insurance Bill

It would be more conducive to the self-respect of the worker that he should derive benefit from a scheme to which he himself was a most substantial contributor. ... I believe that this Bill is setting up a scheme which will be woven into the social fabric of this country, and will be regarded by the working men with gratitude as something which has given them a guarantee with regard to their daily lives. It is a Bill which the employers will accept as something which improves the efficiency of labour and gives stability to the existing order.

From a speech in the House of Commons, 6 December 1911

J Lord Robert Cecil opposes it from the Conservative benches

People bitterly resent in this country being made to apply their own money for benefits in a way they do not approve. ... I have a fanatical belief in individual freedom. I believe it is a vital thing for this country, and I believe it is the cornerstone upon which our prosperity and our existence are built, and, for my part, I believe that the civic qualities of self-control, self-reliance, and self-respect depend upon individual liberty and the freedom and independence of the people of this country.

From a speech in the House of Commons, 6 December 1911

K Labour MP George Lansbury has different objections

Instead of Parliament voting to take away money from people it ought either to be voting to give them money or, what is very much better, it ought to pass some measure of reform which will enable these men and women to earn living wages. ... I am perfectly certain that when you attempt to collect the money you will have just as big a revolt as our forefathers had when they last levied a poll tax in this country. ... I do not understand men who have three or four square meals a day thinking that a man can keep his family in a state of physical efficiency on 7s. a week, and to tell him that it is some great boon you are offering him, to tell him you are offering him something that

43

is going to bring fruit to his parched lips, is really absurd. ... I believe this Bill ... does not touch any root cause at all, either in sickness or in unemployment.

From a speech in the House of Commons, 6 December 1911

L Fabian, Beatrice Webb, has mixed feelings about National Insurance

The plain fact is that Lloyd George and the Radicals have out-trumped the Labour Party. They have dealt out millions of public money. ... The fact that it will be wastefully collected and wastefully spent may condemn it to the thoughtful Socialist or to the economical-minded citizen - but to the ordinary elector it makes no difference since he is too dull witted to understand that it will be so. The big fault of the Act is the creation of huge vested interests ... [which will] mean not only waste of public money and financial chaos ... but wholesale demorali- sation of character through the fraudulent withholding or the fraudulent getting of benefits.

From Beatrice Webb's diary, 1 December 1912

M Lady Desart chairs a meeting of 'respectable' servant-girls and their employers

[National Insurance contributions] would not merely inflict increased hardship on the most defenceless portion of the servant industry; they were calculated to set class against class (cheers) - to prevent in future any approach to friendship, let alone that beautiful intimacy which had hitherto so often existed between mistresses and servants. By what right did Mr. Lloyd George (hisses and laughter) decree that every mistress was to be a tax-gatherer? (Cheers.)

From a report in *The Times*, 30 November 1911

N Medical opposition to the scheme

It is a long step in the downward path towards socialism. It will tend to destroy individual effort, and to increase that spirit of dependency which is ever found in degenerate races. This spoon-fed race will look more and more to a paternal government to feed and clothe it, and not to require it to work more than a few hours daily. They will be further encouraged to multiply their breed at the expense of the healthy and intellectual members of the community. ... Every source of revenue is being tapped for the benefit of the least worthy citizens. Now the medical men are to be sweated in order to provide gratuit- ous medical advice for the least worthy of the wage-earning popula- tion.

From a letter in the *British Medical Journal*, 30 December 1911

O Making hairbrushes in the home. [Pictures like this appeared in the Sweated Industries Exhibition of 1906, which helped to persuade Parliament to pass the Trade Boards Act of 1909 - but this particular trade was not covered by the Act]

P Rowntree reports on the poverty of rural labourers

The be all and end all of [their] life is physical efficiency. ... It means that every natural longing for pleasure or variety should be ignored and set aside. It means, in short, a life without colour, space and atmosphere, that stifles and hems in the labourer's soul, as in too many cases his cottage does his body.

From S. Rowntree and May Kendall: *How the Labourer Lives* (1913)

Q The recorded memories of Leonard Thompson

There were seven children at home and father's wages had been reduced to 10s. a week. Our cottage was nearly empty - except for people. ... There was no newspaper to read and nothing to read except the Bible. All the village houses were like this. Our food was apples, potatoes, swedes and bread, and we drank our tea without milk or sugar. Nobody could get enough to eat no matter how hard they tried. ... In my four months' training with the regiment [he joined the army in March 1914] I put on nearly a stone in weight and got a bit taller. They said it was the food but it was really because for the first time in my life there had been no strenuous work. I want to say this simply as a fact, that village people in Suffolk in my day were worked to death. It literally happened. It is not a figure of speech.

From R. Blythe: *Akenfield: Portrait of an English Village* (1969)

R The Poor Law Commissioners compare reality with Elgar's well-known song

'Land of Hope and Glory' is a popular and patriotic lyric sung each year with rapture by thousands of voices. ... To certain classes of the community into whose moral and material condition it has been our duty to enquire, these words are a mockery and a falsehood. To many of them, possibly from their own failure and faults, there is in this life but little hope, and to many more 'glory' ... is an unknown ideal. Our investigations prove the existence in our midst of a class whose condition and environment are a discredit, and a peril to the whole community. Each and every section of society has a common duty to perform in combating this evil ... a duty which can only be performed by united and untiring effort to convert useless and costly inefficients into self-sustaining and respectable members of the community.

From *Majority Report of the Poor Law Commission* (1909)

S An historian of the 1960s finds the origins of the Welfare State in the Edwardian period

Even before 1945 much had been done, however unsystematically, to advance social welfare. In particular, the foundations of services that were later to expand almost out of recognition were laid in the years from 1906 to 1911. The leading economist of the day, Alfred Marshall, called Lloyd George's Budget of 1909 a 'social welfare budget', and the social purposes of the insurance scheme of 1911, with its contributions from government and employers as well as from the individual worker, were at once recognised in the coining of the phrase 'social insurance'. It was, indeed, both 'social' and 'insurance', both a method of insurance against social ills and, to a very limited extent, a means for the transfer of wealth by taxation for social ends. ... The complicated historical process that has produced the Welfare State in Britain has about it something of a romance. ... We can look back with some satisfaction at the way we have come, even if satisfaction is tempered by the reflection that the way could well have been shorter and straighter.

From M. Bruce: *The Coming of the Welfare State* (1961)

T Thirty years later a different view is expressed

During the debate on National Insurance, the Prime Minister [Asquith] stated that the House was 'conferring upon millions of our fellow-countrymen by the joint operation of self-help and State help, the greatest alleviation of the risks and sufferings of life that Parliament had ever conferred upon any people'. Those who struggled daily with the risks and sufferings of life had good reason to doubt whether either this legislation, or any other reform of the period, measured up to such a claim. ... Despite all the research, all the argument, all the planning and plotting by ministers and their civil servants, all the rhetoric which accompanied each Act onto the Statute Book, the incidence of poverty, and the basic features of the strategies the poor adopted to cope with their problems, changed very little between the end of the Boer War and the outbreak of the Great War. ... The neighbourhood remained for the poor as essential and as inadequate a means of support as it had done in the latter part of the nineteenth century. Pawnbroking reached its peak as the Edwardian period came to an end. ... The concept of 'foundations' which is so often deployed in accounts of the poverty legislation before 1914 is in many ways inaccurate.

From D. Vincent: *Poor Citizens* (1991)

Questions

1 Compare the effectiveness of the different types of Sources used in A, B, C, O, P and Q to convey Edwardian poverty. **(7 marks)**

2 What arguments are employed in Sources D-F for adopting new Liberal policies? **(5 marks)**

3 Compare the attitudes to poor people which are revealed in Sources G-I and R. **(6 marks)**

4 Evaluate the criticisms of the National Insurance scheme advanced in Sources J-N. **(6 marks)**

5 Do you consider Source S or Source T the more valid judgement of the Liberal reforms? **(6 marks)**

5 LIMITING THE LORDS

At the height of the Lords' crisis in 1910, Winston Churchill described an Upper House 'filled with doddering peers, cute financial magnates, clever wire-pullers [and] big brewers with bulbous noses'. Yet this champion of 'the left-out millions' regularly 'weekended' at Blenheim, the country house of his cousin, the Duke of Marlborough. Churchill's 'class treachery' so incensed the Duke of Beaufort that he wanted to see him 'in the middle of twenty couple of dog-hounds' [A].

Churchill's description of the Edwardian peerage may be tendentious but it is not inaccurate. By this time the old landowning caste was merging with the business class. Relative impoverishment, caused by the agricultural depression, had driven many landed families to seek new sources of income by investing in commercial enterprises. On the other hand, increasing numbers of rich businessmen were being ennobled, usually in return for political services (which often took the form of financial contributions to the Conservative or Liberal parties). Among the new lords were familiar names like W.H. Smith, Edward Guinness and Michael Bass. This new 'plutocracy' made itself more socially acceptable by purchasing country estates. There was no shortage of old houses advertised in the new magazine *Country Life*. But the fashionable architect, Sir Edwin Lutyens, was adept at designing harmonious new mansions complete with modern luxuries like garages and swimming-pools. The dilution of the traditional aristocracy enabled it to survive into the twentieth century, but its confidence was weakened even before the parliamentary peers embarked on their disastrous conflict with the Liberals [B-C].

The House of Lords had emerged from the nineteenth century with its composition and powers intact. It consisted of about 570 male hereditary peers (a sixth of whom were first-generation lords) and 26 archbishops and bishops of the Anglican Church. In 1906 there were 355 Conservative members of the House of Lords, 124 Liberal Unionists, 89 Liberals and 35 with no political affiliation. The Lords still had the right to amend or reject bills sent to them by the Commons (though by convention they did not touch money bills). They had exercised this right frequently during nineteenth-century Whig/Liberal ministries and had scored their last victory when they rejected Gladstone's second Home Rule Bill in 1893. Under the Conservative governments which had been in power since 1895 the Upper House had been quiescent, not even seeing fit to interfere with the innovatory Education Act of 1902.

After the Liberal victory of 1906 Balfour encouraged the Conservative peers, led by Lord Lansdowne, to put their majority to use since, he maintained, 'the great Unionist party should still control, whether in power or in opposition, the destinies of this great Empire'. Obediently 'Mr Balfour's poodle' (as Lloyd George dubbed the Upper House) vetoed the Liberals' Education and Licensing Bills. But they astutely refrained from rejecting measures like the Trade Disputes Bill which, as Lord Lansdowne admitted, 'had the approval of working men' [D].

The partisan use of aristocratic power caused many to question the role of hereditary peers in an increasingly democratic constitution and to put forward proposals for reform. Some Conservatives, like Lord Newton in 1907, favoured a less exclusively aristocratic House which should contain life peers appointed by the government of the day. Liberals feared that such a scheme would strengthen the second chamber and Campbell-Bannerman proposed instead that the Lords should be allowed only to delay legislation. Labour wanted to abolish the House of Lords altogether. In the event, the Lords brought about the limitation of their own powers by rejecting the Budget in 1909 [E–F].

Lloyd George regarded this as a 'war budget ... for raising money to wage implacable war against poverty'. In addition he was convinced that the navy needed to be put on a war footing; but there is no evidence that he also intended to make war on the Lords. He proposed higher death duties, a super-tax of 6d in the pound on incomes over £5000, a 20 per cent tax on unearned increase in land values as well as other new land taxes, further duties on alcohol and tobacco and taxation on motor-cars (then luxury items). It is not unusual for those affected by a budget to protest. The Irish leader, John Redmond, condemned the extra halfpenny on a glass of whiskey as unfair to his countrymen. But the 'People's Budget' was seen as such a violent attack on landowners that Balfour and Lord Lansdowne decided on resistance by all means. A Budget Protest League was formed. The Tories held up the Budget for 70 days of exhausting debate in the Commons. And when it reached the Upper House in the autumn the peers rejected it by 350 votes to 75. Since the government had thus been denied the supply of money needed for its programme, Asquith had no choice but to dissolve Parliament [G–I].

In the election which followed in January 1910, the Conservatives proposed tariff reform as their alternative to punitive taxes. They gained 100 seats, winning about the same number as the Liberals who retained power only with Irish and Labour support. Urged on by its political allies as well as by its own supporters, Asquith's new government embarked on a scheme to abolish the Lords' veto. In the words of Redmond, this would be 'tantamount to the granting of Home Rule to Ireland' [K].

Reluctantly conceding defeat, the Lords passed the Budget in April. By then the government was pushing a Parliament Bill through the Commons. It stipulated that the Lords could neither reject nor amend money bills and that other bills would become law despite the Lords' opposition if the Commons passed them three times. To make the Commons more accountable to the electorate (which still comprised only 58 per cent of the adult male population), general elections were to be held at intervals of five rather than seven years. Anticipating that the Upper House would throw out this bill, Asquith had already approached Edward VII with a view to his using the royal prerogative to create large numbers of Liberal peers who would let it through. Apart from this, Asquith's policy was, in his own words, to 'wait and see'.

The crisis was prolonged by the death of the King in May, 1910. Asquith called a Constitutional Conference to try to resolve the matter and thus save the new King, George V, the embarrassment of coercing the Upper House. This came to nothing, however, and the King (in the words of his diary) 'agreed most reluctantly ... to make peers if asked for'. In November the Lords duly rejected the Parliament Bill and a second general election took place in December [J-K].

Another extremely close result enabled Conservatives to claim that the Liberals had no popular mandate for limiting the Lords' power. While the second Parliament Bill made its contested way through the Commons, Lord Lansdowne vainly put forward alternative proposals to reconstitute and strengthen his Chamber. When the Parliament Bill at last came before the Lords in June they amended it beyond all recognition. But noble resistance began to falter when Balfour and Lansdowne found out about the King's promise to flood the Upper House with new peers. Asquith had gone so far as to prepare a list, which included such eminent Edwardians as Thomas Hardy, Bertrand Russell, James Barrie and General Baden-Powell. During a summer in which both meteorological and political temperatures soared the Lords split into 'hedgers', who were now prepared to surrender, and 'ditchers', who were determined to fight to the last ditch. The final debate took place in August when the Parliament Bill was passed by a narrow majority, with 300 peers abstaining [L-O].

This protracted crisis used up so much parliamentary time that the Liberals' legislative programme was wrecked; Churchill's proposals for a fairer penal system, for instance, had to be dropped. The crisis also caused the resignation of Balfour, whose vacillation had helped to divide his party. In the years before the First World War, the Lords wielded their delaying power against Welsh Disestablishment (which was not therefore enacted until 1920) and, of course, against Irish Home Rule [Chapter 8]. The intention announced in the preamble of the Parliament Act to make the House of Lords 'popular' rather than 'hereditary' has not been fulfilled, though there are now life peers as well as those with inherited titles. An aristocratic House of Parliament, similar to the one caricatured by Churchill in 1910, has survived into the late twentieth century.

A The Duke of Marlborough's first wife describes a typical dinner for weekend guests at Blenheim

On the second evening a gilt service would adorn the table and it blended well with the soft mauve and white of a magnificent display of orchids from the hothouses. ... We had a good chef but there had to be perfect co-ordination with the butler in order to serve an eight-course dinner within the hour we had prescribed as the time limit. ... Two soups, one hot and one cold, were served simultaneously. Then came two fish, again one hot and one cold, with accompanying sauces. I still remember my intense annoyance with a very greedy man who complained bitterly that both his favourite fish were being served and that he wished to eat both, so that I had to keep the service waiting while he consumed first the hot and then the cold, quite unperturbed at the delay he was causing. An entree was succeeded by a meat dish. Sometimes a sorbet preceded the game, which in the shooting season was varied, comprising grouse, partridge, pheasant, duck, woodcock and snipe. ... An elaborate sweet followed, succeeded by a hot savoury with which was drunk the port so comforting to English palates. The dinner ended with a succulent array of peaches, plums, apricots, nectarines, strawberries, raspberries, pears and grapes, all grouped in generous pyramids among the flowers that adorned the table.

From Consuelo Balsan: *The Glitter and the Gold* (1952)

B H.G. Wells describes the country house bought by his fictitious character, George Ponderevo [who has made a fortune out of a bogus patent medicine]

Lady Grove is a very beautiful house indeed, a still and gracious place, whose age-old seclusion was only effectively broken with the toot of the coming of the motor-car. ... Portions of the fabric are thirteenth century, and its last architectural revision was Tudor; within it is for the most part dark and chilly, save for two or three favoured rooms and its tall-windowed, oak-galleried hall. Its terrace is its noblest feature ... southward one looks down upon the tops of wayfaring trees and spruces, and westward on a steep slope of beechwood. ... One turns back to the still old house, and one sees a gray and lichenous facade with a very finely arched entrance. It was warmed by the afternoon light and touched with the colour of a few neglected roses and pyracanthus. ... And there was my uncle holding his [motoring] goggles in a sealskin glove, wiping the glass with a pocket-handkerchief, and asking my aunt if Lady Grove wasn't 'A bit of all Right.'

[Later Ponderevo suggests that he might enter the peerage]

'It's a wonderful system - this old British system. It's staid and stable, and yet it has place for new men. We come up and take our places. It's almost expected. We take a hand. That's where our Democracy differs from America. Over there a man succeeds; all he gets is money. Here there's a system - open to everyone - practically. ... Chaps like Lord Boom - come from nowhere.'

From H.G. Wells: *Tono-Bungay* (1909)

C The Hall at Kinloch Castle [furnished with the dead for the dubious comfort of the living]

D Arthur Balfour writes privately to Lord Lansdowne about Conservative strategy

The real point is ... to secure that the party in the two Houses shall not work as two separate armies, but shall co-operate in a common plan of campaign. ... There has certainly never been a period in our history in which the House of Lords will be called upon to play a part at once so important, so delicate, and so difficult. I do not think the House of Lords will be able to escape the duty of making serious modifications in important Government measures, but, if this is done with caution and tact, I do not believe that they will do themselves any harm. On the contrary, as the rejection of the Home Rule Bill undoubtedly strengthened their position, I think it is quite possible that your House may come out of the ordeal strengthened rather than weakened by the inevitable difficulties of the next few years.

From a memorandum by Balfour, 13 April 1906

E Campbell-Bannerman comments on the Lords' rejection of the Liberals' Education Bill

Now the question we have to ask ourselves is - Is the general election and its result to go for nothing? ... It is plainly intolerable, Sir, that a second Chamber should, while one party in the State is in power, be its willing servant, and when that party has received an unmistakable and emphatic condemnation by the country, the House of Lords should be able to neutralize, thwart, and distort the policy which the electors have approved. ... But, Sir, the resources of the British Constitution are not wholly exhausted ... and I say with conviction that a way must be found, a way will be found, by which the will of the people expressed through their elected representatives in this House will be made to prevail.

From a speech in the House of Commons, 20 December 1906

F Labour MP, Arthur Henderson, expresses a radical solution

I hope that the Government, having set out to bring about a reform of the intolerable position they are now in, will carry the issue right to the finish. On this question the Labour Party want no patchwork. We will never consent to a reform which might leave us with a second Chamber in existence that makes the last position worse than the first. That being so, we go in for ending instead of mending the House of Lords.

[Later in the year Henderson formally proposed that] The Upper House, being an irresponsible part of the Legislature, and of necessity representative only of interests opposed to the general well-being, is a hindrance to national progress and ought to be abolished.

From speeches in the House of Commons, 18 February and 25 June 1907

G Lloyd George justifies the right to tax owners of lucrative land in the London Docks

Who created that increment? Who made that golden swamp? Was it the landlord? Was it *his* energy? Was it *his* brains? - a very bad look out if it were! - his foresight? It was purely the combined efforts of the people engaged in the trade and commerce of the Port of London - trader, merchant, dock labourer, workman, everybody *except* the landlord. ... Now that is coming to an end. In future those landlords will have to contribute to the taxation of the country on the basis of the real values. ... Take cases like Golder's Green, where the land has gone up in the course, perhaps of a couple of years, through a new tramway or a new railway being opened. A few years ago there was a plot of land at Golder's Green which was sold at £160. Last year I went and opened a Tube railway there. ... What was the result? This year that very piece of land has been sold for £2,000. ... My Budget demands 20 per cent of that. ... We are placing burdens on the broadest shoulders. Why should *I* put burdens on the people? I am one of the children of the people. (Loud and prolonged cheering.) I was brought up among them. I know their trials; and God forbid that I should add one grain of trouble to the anxieties which they bear with such patience and fortitude.

From a speech by Lloyd George at Limehouse, 30 July 1909

H   Lord Lansdowne urges the Lords to reject the Budget so that it can be 'referred to the people'
Is this an ordinary budget? His Majesty's ministers have never ceased explaining that it is anything but an ordinary budget. Take the language of the Prime Minister a few weeks ago in the City. He spoke of the budget as having 'far-reaching political and social results' - political and social, mind you, not financial. ... It is idle to talk of the bill as being an ordinary Budget Bill. ... These [land] taxes are justifiable if you believe that land is national property, and that it should be the business of Parliament to nationalise the land.

From a speech in the House of Lords, 22 November 1909

I   Asquith argues that the House of Lords must be reformed
For what is our actual Second Chamber? It is a body which has no pretensions or qualifications to be the organ or the interpreter of the popular will. It is a body in which one party of State is in possession of a permanent and an overwhelming majority. It is a body which, as experience shows, in temper and in action, is frankly and nakedly partisan. It is a body which does not attempt to exercise any kind of effective control over the legislation of the other House when its own party is in a majority there. It is a body which, when the conditions are reversed, however clear and emphatic the verdict of the country may have been, sets itself to work to mutilate and to obstruct democratic legislation and even, in these last days, to usurp the control of the democratic finance. ... We are not proposing the abolition of the House of Lords or setting up a single Chamber, but we do ask ... the electors to say that the House of Lords shall be confined to the proper functions of a Second Chamber. The absolute veto which it at present possesses must go. ... The people in future when they elect a new House of Commons, must be able to feel, what they cannot feel now, that they are sending to Westminster men who will have the power not merely of proposing and debating, but of

making laws. The will of the people, as expressed by their elected representatives, must within the limits of a single Parliament, be made effective.

From an election speech at the Albert Hall, 10 December 1910

J   A typical Budget Protest League Poster

K The results of the two 1910 elections

	Votes	Seats	Percentage Vote
Jan-Feb election			
Conservative	3,127,887	273	46.9
Liberal	2,880,581	275	43.2
Labour	511,392	40	7.7
Irish Party	124,586	82	1.9
Others	22,958	0	0.3
Electorate	7,694,741		
Turnout	86.6%		
December election			
Conservatives	2,424,566	272	46.3
Liberal	2,293,686	272	43.8
Labour	376,581	42	7.2
Irish Party	131,721	84	2.5
Others	8,768	0	0.2
Electorate	7,709,981		
Turnout	81.1%		

From D. Butler & J. Freeman: *British Political Facts* (1963)

L Balfour favours retaining the second chamber's power to check 'the uncontrolled licence' of all governments

We live under a representative party system [which] always tends to work out into something like rough equality between the two opposing camps. ... When the election is over and all this hurling and crushing is finished, you will find that the people who are in the minority are a fraction less than half the voters, and the people who are in power are a fraction more than half the voters - and not a very big fraction. ... However big the majority may be - take, for example, that which destroyed the Unionist Government in 1906 - even at that time you will find that those who suffered that defeat have behind them a vast body of their countrymen, and those not the least intelligent! ... I think it is utterly absurd to say that the transfer of these few votes at a General Election under the violent impulse of some hope, fear, or passion of the moment, is to give a universal Power-of-Attorney to any Government to do exactly what it likes with the British Constitution.

From a speech in the House of Commons, 2 March 1911

M The Duke of Northumberland defends the powers of his chamber

We represent, my Lords, in a peculiar degree the education and the intelligence of the country. ... Not only that, but this House represents in a peculiar way the property, the wealth of the country - that property which it is necessary to preserve, and which the tendency of all democracies is to attack, and which the end of all democracies is to annihilate. ... In the case of the great majority of your Lordships you did not seek the position which you occupy. It has been conferred upon you by Providence, and you are responsible to the source from which you derive it for the exercise which you make of your opportunities. The experience of ages has shown that the powers possessed by this House are essential to the liberties of the people, and a necessary safeguard against violent and confiscatory legislation. Those safeguards were never more necessary than now. According to my best judgement, we have no right by any act of omission or commission to jeopardise them, but, on the contrary, to hand them down, if possible, intact to future generations.

From a speech in the House of Lords, 24 May 1911

N In a speech peppered with the word 'forsooth' the aged Earl of Halsbury urges peers to fight on
I myself certainly will not yield to the threat. Let the Government take the responsibility of introducing 400 or 500 peers - I care not how many - in the circumstances that my noble friend [Lord Lansdowne] has pointed out and then let him shield himself by saying 'And you forced them to do it'. I never heard such an extraordinary argument in my life. It is as if a highwayman came and said, 'Give me your watch or I cut your throat', and if you did not give him your watch that you are the author of your own throat being cut. ... Nothing in the world would induce me not to vote against a Bill which I believe to be wrong and immoral and a scandalous example of legislation.

From a speech in the House of Lords, 9 August 1911

O In heat so intense as to cause his normally immaculate collar to dissolve, Lord Curzon puts the 'hedger' case
What good will you do to yourselves, to your party, to the Constitution, to the country, or to anyone concerned? ... I truly think that nothing more ridiculous, more open to the charge of contempt, could be imagined than this creation of Peers; but at the bottom of my heart I cannot help thinking that the country ... so far from believing that His Majesty's Government had resorted to an action which is ridiculous, would say that the Peers, who had stood out twice against His Majesty's Government and had been defeated, were finally being hoisted with their own petard. ... I cannot contemplate with satisfaction anything which must effect the pollution - perhaps that is too strong a word - the degradation of this House, and I ask your Lordships to pause before you not only acquiesce in, but precipitate or facilitate, a course ... which cannot but have the effect of covering this House with ridicule and of destroying its power for good in the future.

From a speech in the House of Lords, 10 August 1911

Questions

1 What impressions do you gain of Edwardian upper-class life from Sources A-C? **(6 marks)**

2 Compare the different views of the future role of the House of Lords which are expressed in Sources D-F. **(5 marks)**

3 In the light of Sources G, H and J (and your own knowledge) do you think it was appropriate for the *Daily Mail* to call Lloyd George's 1909 Budget 'the production of wild socialists'? **(6 marks)**

4 How helpful are the figures in Source K for evaluating the different interpretations of democracy in Sources I, L and M? **(7 marks)**

5 In the light of Sources N and O explain why the House of Lords allowed the Parliament Bill to pass. **(6 marks)**

6 DEFENDING THE WORKERS

'The House of Commons is supposed to be the people's House, and yet the people are not there. Landlords, employers, lawyers, brewers and financiers are there in force. Why not Labour?' Notwithstanding this proletarian plea, there were actually a few working-class MPs in the late Victorian age. But they were radical Liberals, often standing with trade union support, known as 'Lib-Labs'. In 1892, however, James Keir Hardie was elected as an independent. He was an illegitimate Scottish miner who had started work in the pits at the age of eight and was determined that 'the wants and wishes of the working classes shall be made known and attended to in Parliament'. So in 1893 he established the Independent Labour Party [ILP]. It was socialist and aimed to place land, industry and capital under 'collective ownership'. This did not appeal to the trade unions, whose purpose was simply to improve wages and working conditions. Yet without the support of the unions' substantial funds and their two million members the ILP could make little headway.

In spite of their misgivings about socialism, trade unionists gradually became convinced that they must have a body of reliable MPs to defend their rights. This was because the position of the unions was weakening. Employers were banding together, using non-union labour to break strikes, 'locking out' workers who made demands and appealing successfully in the courts against the unions' right to picket. Thus in 1900 trade union delegates agreed with the ILP and other socialist societies to set up the Labour Representation Committee [LRC], which would work to create 'a distinct Labour group in Parliament'. At this time no specific policies were spelt out. Individual unions were slow to affiliate with the LRC until the Taff Vale case provided an added incentive. After a strike by its employees the Taff Vale Railway Company sued the rail union for damages and, in December 1902, it was awarded £23,000 plus costs. This decision set a precedent and, unless reversed by act of parliament, would make strikes almost impossible. Since the Conservatives were hostile and the Liberals were split over the Boer War, the unions' best hope for legislation lay in supporting a Labour party [A-B].

By 1903 there were 8500 trade union members of the LRC, which now had an annual income of £5000 and a fund with which to pay MPs. It was further strengthened by a secret pact with the Liberal Party: in return for Labour support if they won the next election, the Liberals promised not to fight in certain constituencies where the LRC was standing. This agreement proved helpful to both sides in the 1906 election, at which 29

LRC candidates were returned. When the new parliament assembled they emphasised their separate status by sitting on the opposition benches and giving themselves a new name. Thus the Labour Party came into being and elected Keir Hardie as its first leader [C].

This small group of MPs managed to influence Campbell-Bannerman's government. It amended the Liberals' cautious Trade Disputes Bill of 1906 so as to reverse the Taff Vale decision: the Act prevented unions from being sued for damages and confirmed that peaceful picketing was legal. The Labour Party also improved the Workmen's Compensation Act so that it gave a further six million workers protection. And it was a Labour bill which introduced school meals for needy children.

In 1909 a group of 15 Lib-Lab MPs backed by the miners' unions joined the Labour Party, which by this time was having less success. It was unhappy with the Old Age Pensions Act and the National Insurance Act [Chapter 4]. Also a Labour bill to give unemployed people the right to work had been rejected. Although there were still 42 Labour MPs after the two elections of 1910, their influence on the Liberal government waned as that of the vociferous Irish Nationalists waxed. Thus Labour (now led by Ramsay MacDonald) found itself supporting traditionally Liberal legislation (like the disestablishment of the Anglican Church in Wales) rather than initiating reforms to improve working-class life. Its weakness is illustrated by the Osborne case of 1909, in which the Court of Appeal ruled that it was illegal for trade unions to use members' subscriptions to support the Labour Party. The damage was partly alleviated by the payment of salaries (£400 a year) to MPs after 1911, but not until 1913 did the government find time to pass an act legalising the use of trade union funds for political purposes. Even then Labour MPs were unhappy with the clause which allowed trade union members to contract out of the political part of the subscription.

By 1914 the Labour Party had been reduced to 36 MPs after a series of unsuccessful by-elections. Labour's disappointing performance has been explained in various ways. The Liberals had to some extent taken the wind out of Labour sails before 1911 and after that they were too preoccupied to heed Labour. Beatrice Webb accused trade union MPs of being 'stolid, stupid folk' and historians tend to agree that they lacked political expertise. The Labour Party was also increasingly divided, especially over how far it should espouse socialism [D-E].

The Labour Party's shortcomings encouraged workers to resort to extra-parliamentary methods. Strikes increased sharply between 1910 and 1914. Upper- and middle-class contemporaries tended to blame the industrial unrest on Syndicalism - the belief that workers could gain control of industry by means of militant and concerted action. Syndicalist ideas were popular among some workers but historians find that their influence did not run very deep. Another explanation for the strikes is that they were a reaction against falling 'real wages'. In fact, as recent economic historians have suggested, wages just about kept pace with prices. What strikers wanted above all was 'a living wage' - one on which they could do more than simply survive [G-J].

The strikes worried the government greatly, particularly because they coincided with the House of Lords conflict, suffragette militancy, the Irish Home Rule crisis and mounting tension in Europe. Liberal cabinet ministers were reluctant to abandon *laissez-faire* policies but found that they had to intervene. They relied heavily on Lloyd George's consummate negotiating skills and on G.R. Askwith, the Board of Trade official who acted as conciliator in every dispute. Controversy still surrounds the frequent use of troops, for which Winston Churchill as Home Secretary was responsible. The first instance of this occurred in 1910 during a ten-month strike by miners in South Wales. After violent clashes between strikers and police at Tonypandy the Chief Constable sent for military help. It was only after continued riots, during which one man was killed, that Churchill sent a detachment of soldiers. He has been bitterly attacked for his intervention at Tonypandy (both at the time and since) but records reveal that his aim was to prevent bloodshed rather than to crush the strike by force. The summer of 1911 brought strikes by seamen, dockers and railwaymen, who threatened to bring the country to a standstill. The record August heat and the alarm caused by the Agadir crisis added to the tension [Chapter 9]. To protect strike-breaking workers Churchill sent troops to various parts of the country. During riots in Liverpool they killed one man and at Llanelly they shot two more. After this Lloyd George quickly found a compromise between the rail owners and their employees [J-K].

In 1912 the situation became even more critical: a record 41 million days were lost by strike action. Asquith was so concerned about the national coal strike between February and April that he rushed an act through Parliament establishing boards to fix district minimum wages, a measure which fell short of the national guaranteed wage demanded by miners. There followed another strike by London dockworkers, during which their leader Ben Tillett prayed: 'O God, strike Lord Devonport dead!' The Chairman of the London Port Authority survived but the strike collapsed, largely because it did not gain the support of other workers. To increase their bargaining power, dockers, miners and railwaymen formed a 'triple alliance' in 1914. With trade union membership now topping four million, industrial strife seemed to be reaching a climax. However, soon after the outbreak of the First World War trade unions proclaimed a truce in the class war: they encouraged members to defend 'King and Country'. Their sacrifice was rewarded. Ironically, the global conflict did as much to strengthen both trade unions and the Labour Party as did the efforts of their Edwardian leaders [L-N].

A   Richard Bell, Secretary of the rail union and an LRC MP, argues against the Taff Vale decision

What we complain of is that the new interpretation put on the law by the judges is all in favour of the employers. ... During the progress of the Taff Vale strike, two men interfered with the working of a train - a most deplorable thing to do - an act condemned by me and all sensible people. These men were arrested, they were tried at the assizes, and were sentenced to six weeks' imprisonment with hard labour. They deserved all they got. ... But the employers now come, because of the action of these men, to claim damages from the union. I say it is monstrous, and it was never intended to be part of the law. ... What we desire is that the Government should bring in a bill to restore the unions to the position in which they were by the Acts previous to the decision of the House of Lords, or at least to put them on a fair and equal footing with the employers. ... I venture to say that the two millions of Trade Unionists of this country will not consent to remain in their present position.

From a speech in the House of Commons, 14 May 1902

B   A Labour poster draws attention to trade union grievances

C An extract from the LRC's 1906 election manifesto

The Trade Unions ask the same liberty as capital enjoys. They are refused.

The aged poor are neglected.

The slums remain; overcrowding continues, while the land goes to waste.

Shopkeepers and traders are overburdened with rates and taxation, whilst the increasing land values, which should relieve the rate-payers, go to people who have not earned them.

Wars are fought to make the rich richer, and the underfed school children are still neglected. ...

The unemployed ask for work, the Government gave them a worthless Act. And now, when you are beginning to understand the causes of your poverty, the red herring of Protection is drawn across your path.

From the manifesto of the Labour Representation Committee, 1906

D Ben Tillett, leader of the dockers' union, denounces the Labour Party's support for Liberal causes

I do not hesitate to describe the conduct of these blind leaders as nothing short of betrayal especially with the fact in view they have displayed greater activity for temperance reform than for Labour interests. ... The worst of the winter is coming on, time thrown away will never be recovered, and thousands will perish for want of bread. A great many of the victims of destitution will be in their graves before the Liberal Government will have approached the subject of unemployment, which they will sandwich between abolition of the House of Lords and Welsh Disestablishment. The temperance section, in particular, will be seizing on other 'red-herrings', and the winter will have passed, and these unctuous weaklings will go on prattling their nonsense, while thousands are dying of starvation. ... Blessed, valuable months have been lost; the Labour movement must not tolerate the further betrayal of interests with agitations about the House of Lords, or Welsh Disestablishment.

From B. Tillett: *Is the Parliamentary Labour Party a Failure?* (1908)

E Beatrice Webb comments on Labour's growing weakness

July 5th 1913 The Parliamentary Labour Party is ... in a bad way ... [and] has not justified its existence either by character or by intelligence, and it is doubtful whether it will hold the Trade Unions. The Labour and Socialist Movement is in a state of disruption, there is more evil speaking and suspicion than there has ever been before, and there is less enthusiasm.

February 6th 1914 The Labour Party Conference was a personal triumph for MacDonald. ... With his romantic figure, charming voice and clever dialectics [argument], [he] is more than a match for all those underbred and under-trained workmen who surround him on the platform and face him in the audience. ... In his old-fashioned Radicalism - in his friendliness to Lloyd George - he represents the views and aspirations of the bulk of Trade Unionists. ... The British Workman has been persuaded by the propaganda of the ILP that a Labour Party is useful, that some of his class ought to enjoy the £400 a year and the prestige of the MP's position, but the closer the Labour Member sticks to the Liberal Party the better he is pleased. So far as he has any politics he still believes in the right of the middle and professional classes to do the work of government. He does not believe his own mates are capable of it, and roughly speaking he is right.

From Beatrice Webb's Diary

F   The rapid rise in trade union activity

	Total union membership	Number of stoppages beginning in year	Total working days lost in year
1907	2,513,000	585	2,150,000
1910	2,565,000	521	9,870,000
1911	3,139,000	872	10,160,000
1912	3,416,000	834	40,890,000
1913	4,135,000	1,459	9,800,000
1914	4,145,000	972	9,880,000

From D. Read (ed.): *Edwardian England* (1982)

G   The objectives of Syndicalist miners in South Wales
We cannot get rid of employers and slave-driving in the mining industry, until all other industries have organized for, and progressed towards, the same objective ... all we can do is to set an example and the pace. ...

Our objective begins to take shape before your eyes. Every industry thoroughly organised, in the first place, to fight, to gain control of, and then to administer, that industry. The co-ordination of all industries on a Central Production Board, who, with a statistical department to ascertain the needs of the people, will issue its demands on the different departments of industry, leaving the men themselves to determine under what conditions and how, the work should be done. This would mean real democracy in real life, making for real manhood and womanhood. Any other form of democracy is a delusion and a snare.

From a pamphlet *The Miners' Next Step* (1912)

H A.L. Bowley's contemporary statistics on real wages have been challenged by Charles Feinstein, a modern economic historian

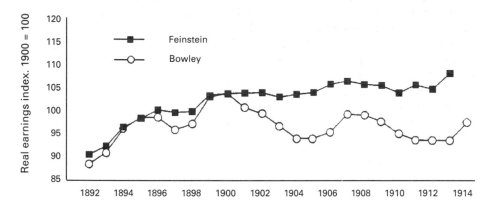

from P. Johnson (ed.): *Twentieth Century Britain: Economic, Social and Cultural Change* (1994)

I A Labour MP explains what is meant by a 'living wage'
There has been an advance in the cost of living in another sense than by the increase in the price of commodities. New expenses have come into the category of necessities. The development of tramways, the coming of the halfpenny newspaper, the cheap but better-class music hall and the picture palace, the cheap periodicals and books, the very municipal enterprise which was intended to provide free libraries, free parks, free concerts, has added to the expenditure of the working classes, who cannot take advantage of these boons without incurring some little expense in sundries. The features of our advancing civilisation are always before the eyes of the working classes, and they fall into the habit of indulging in the cheaper ones. People cannot see tramways without wanting to ride sometimes; they cannot see newspapers without at least buying one occasionally; they cannot see others taking a holiday into the country or to the seaside without desiring to do the same. These additional items of working class expenditure, coming out of wages which are stationary, make the struggle to live more intense, and compel a lessening of expenditure on absolute necessaries.

From P. Snowden: *The Living Wage* (1913)

J Keir Hardie argues that troops committed murder at Llanelly
A train was stopped by a crowd of strikers squatting down on the line in front of it. Some troops, quartered at the station, rushed up at the double, and lined up on both sides of the engine. ... The train was standing in a deep cutting, and the official story is that stones were

coming in showers from both sides. Now, not one pane of glass in the carriage windows was broken, not one passenger was hurt or molested, in fact they were looking out of the windows, no civilian was struck, no property was damaged; there was no riot. But the officer in command ordered the people to disperse; he gave them one minute in which to do so; at the end of the minute he ordered five shots to be fired which killed two men outright, and wounded four others. John Jones, one of the murdered men, was sitting on the garden wall of his own house in shirt and trousers, looking on; the other was also in his garden at the top of the railway embankment. ... Presumably they made good targets, and so were picked off ... [The troops'] instructions were to shoot to kill.

From K. Hardie: *Killing No Murder* (1911)

K A note by Churchill defends his use of troops during the rail strike
The progress of a democratic country is bound up with the maintenance of order. The working classes would be almost the only sufferers from an outbreak of riot & a general strike if it cd be effective would fall upon them & their families with its fullest severity. At the same time the wages now paid are too low and the rise in the cost of living ... makes it absolutely necessary that they shd. be raised. I have never heard of the British people complaining (as they now do) without a good & just cause.

Churchill to the Manchester Liberal Party, 5 September 1911

L A churchman describes the plight of striking dockers' families
It is impossible for the outside world to realise all the ghastly horror of this strike. The people are literally starving to death by thousands. They have pawned everything they possess in the world and have nothing to do but sit at home and starve. I could take you to homes where everything has been sold and the members of the family crouch on the floor and watch each other starve. They have nothing left to buy food with, no clothes to go out in, and no furniture and no fuel. ... They just sit on the floor in speechless despair, day and night, waiting for something to come and end it all. ... It was only the other day that I saw one wretched mother begging feverishly that a pawnbroker should give her twopence for two little glass vases. They were all she had left and she wanted to buy two cods' heads with the twopence to keep her children alive a little longer.

From a *Daily Express* report by Dean Ring of St Mary and St Michael's, 1912

M Lenin sees the miners' strike as a prelude to revolution
The miners' strike was the outstanding event of the past year. While the railway strike in 1911 showed the 'new spirit' of the British

workers, the miners' strike marked an epoch. ... The British proletariat is *no longer the same*. The workers have learned to fight. They have come to see the *path* that will lead them to victory. They have become aware of their strength. They have ceased to be the meek lambs they seemed to be for so long a time to the joy of all the defenders and extollers of wage-slavery. In Britain a change has taken place in the balance of social forces.

From an article in *Pravda*, 1912

N   Historian Paul Thompson has a different view
Had the labour unrest been met by unbending coercion and resistance, it could well have proved a revolutionary movement. ... The governing classes neither proved intransigent nor collapsed. Nor did the working classes as a whole become socialist. ... The industrial militancy was never effectively carried over into political consciousness. [One explanation is that] the support found in many of the chapels for the labour cause ... tended to limit working-class consciousness. This was true even of the socialists. Many of them shared Nonconformist beliefs in the path of self-improvement through thrift and temperance. ... The dominant strain in the Edwardian socialist movement [was] an emphasis on understanding and brotherhood, on class solidarity rather than class conflict. ... And another [influence] may perhaps be found in the rising common culture of the music halls and cinemas, with its tolerance, its evasion of political and religious disputes, and its fatalism: the culture of Dan Leno and Charlie Chaplin - of little men chased by angry women and giant foremen.

From P. Thompson: *The Edwardians* (1992)

Questions

1 How far do Sources A and B explain the first point in Source C?
(6 marks)

2 To what extent do Sources D and E explain the Labour Party's failure to secure fully the other promises in Source C?   **(6 marks)**

3 What different motives for the industrial unrest shown in Source F are illustrated in Sources G–I?   **(6 marks)**

4 Which of Sources J–L conveys most reliably the suffering with which strikes were accompanied?   **(6 marks)**

5 How useful are Sources M and N in judging the likelihood of revolution at this time?   **(6 marks)**

7 EMANCIPATING WOMEN

'Man for the field and woman for the hearth:
Man for the sword and for the needle she:
Man with the head and woman with the heart:
Man to command and woman to obey;
All else confusion.'

Thus Tennyson defined the ideal role of Victorian women in society
and in the home. In the early twentieth century the prevailing view was
still that women should be subordinate to men but 'confusion' arose
as women and men began to question that assumption [A-B].

Even in Tennyson's day his ideal of genteel womanhood had been
belied by the thousands of women in working-class occupations - though
those in domestic service or dressmaking might, unwittingly, have fitted
it. By Edwardian times it was becoming much more common for
educated girls to follow middle-class careers as schoolteachers, nurses,
civil servants or secretaries, though they received much lower salaries
than their male counterparts. But ladies still did not work: Lady Violet
Bonham-Carter was told that after her education she was to 'do *nothing*'.

Women generally left their jobs when they got married; they became
responsible for the household and for child-rearing. Their duties were
often onerous, especially in families without servants. Married women
had gained more rights in the late nineteenth century: they could now
own property, sue for maintenance if their husbands deserted them and
sometimes gain custody of their children. But wives remained subordinate to their husbands, though a few daring 'new women' were
rebelling against this convention or even questioning the institution of
marriage itself. As it happened, the growing sexual imbalance in the
population meant that more women were destined to be spinsters. Could
they lead independent lives as single working women or were they to be
pitied as 'the unenjoyed' and derided as redundant to society? The
Edwardians were not at all sure [C-G].

Since 1869, women (more often single than married) who were
householders in their own right had been entitled to vote in local
elections. Now that they were having fewer children, middle-class women
also participated more in public life, sitting on school boards, managing
the Poor Law, and running religious organisations like the Mothers'
Union. In so far as these activities were concerned with children, charity
and church they were accepted as a natural extension of the domestic

role. Inevitably they led to more political involvement. In the 1880s the Liberal and Conservative parties formed women's branches which were generally content, as Mrs Gladstone put it, 'to help our husbands'. Some women, though, began to demand full political rights for themselves and to join suffrage societies, which merged in 1897 to form the National Union of Women's Suffrage Societies (NUWSS) under the leadership of Millicent Fawcett. Its aim was to demand the suffrage 'as it is, and may be given to men'. The peaceful methods of the NUWSS had achieved no parliamentary success by 1903 when Emmeline Pankhurst attacked it as 'incorrigibly leisurely' and, with her daughters Sylvia and Christabel, set up the more forceful Women's Social and Political Union (WSPU). Both organisations saw the suffrage as a means of gaining reforms which would benefit those who gained the vote. The main difference between the NUWSS and the WSPU arose from the latter's early adoption of militant methods. Meanwhile most women remained unconcerned with such unfeminine matters and some were actively hostile to the derisively nicknamed 'suffragettes' [H-K].

Over the next ten years the confusion predicted by Tennyson reigned both in Parliament and in the suffrage societies. Most Liberal MPs and some cabinet ministers differed from their leader, Asquith, in that they supported women's suffrage in principle. The problem was to decide which women should vote. Liberals were reluctant to extend the existing male qualification to women since this would enfranchise only female householders - who would tend to vote Conservative. On the other hand schemes for radical franchise reform, covering the excluded 40 per cent of men as well as women, stood little chance of success without the backing of the Prime Minister. After the failure of various private members' bills, Mrs Pankhurst was prepared by 1910 to abandon the working-class women she had championed earlier and to settle for an all-party compromise in the form of a Conciliation Bill, giving the vote to female occupiers of property. Although many MPs thought that it was better than nothing, the Bill could not weather the political storms of those years without government support and in 1912 it foundered. The next year, a Franchise Bill proposing universal manhood suffrage was withdrawn by the Speaker when it became clear that the Commons would probably pass an amendment to include females. Though Asquith was happy about the withdrawal there is no evidence that, as furious suffragists believed, he had engineered it. With the defeat of a further private member's bill in 1913 there was stalemate [L-N].

There was even more disarray in the suffrage societies. In the face of political failure the WSPU resorted to ever more militant tactics. They interrupted political meetings and parliamentary debates, smashed windows, burned buildings, slashed pictures, despoiled golf-courses, chained themselves to railings and committed many other outrages.

When arrested and imprisoned women used the hunger strike as a further weapon. The authorities resorted to forcible feeding, which was condemned as barbarous. So in 1913 Parliament passed the 'Cat and Mouse' Act, thus called because it allowed prisoners weakened by starvation to be released and later recalled to prison. The publicity which these methods gave to the cause led to a great increase in membership both of the WSPU and of the NUWSS, which continued to oppose militancy. On the other hand, the Women's Anti-Suffrage League, set up in 1909, also attracted much support. Meanwhile the use of violence and the dictatorial direction of the campaign by Mrs Pankhurst led to splits in the WSPU in 1907 and 1913. Even Sylvia Pankhurst, upset by the increasingly conservative, middle-class and anti-male tone of her mother and sister, was forced out of the Union in 1914 [O-P].

It is difficult to know whether violence helped or hindered the cause. Historians tend to conclude that, though the outrages made Asquith's opposition easier and that of potential supporters like Lloyd George more difficult, they cannot be blamed for women's failure to gain the vote before the war. This was due rather to the generally unfavourable political climate of those years. In 1918, however, Parliament rapidly passed a Bill giving the vote to female occupiers of property who were over 30. The measure succeeded not only because women had contributed valiantly to the war effort but also because suffragette militancy had ensured that the issue could not be ignored. Ironically, as women went to the polls for the first time they meekly gave up to returning soldiers the jobs which they had been called upon to perform during the war. Thus they returned to the hearth and the needle - but not usually to the unquestioning obedience described by Tennyson [Q-R].

A   John Ruskin explains the proper functions of the sexes

The man's power is active, progressive, defensive. He is eminently the doer, the creator, the discoverer, the defender. His intellect is for speculation and invention; his energy for adventure, for war, and for conquest wherever war is just, wherever conquest necessary. But the woman's power is for rule, not for battle, - and her intellect is not for invention or creation, but for the sweet ordering, arrangement, and decision. ... By her office, and place, she is protected from all danger and temptation. ... This is the true nature of home - it is the place of Peace; the shelter, not only from all injury, but from all terror, doubt, and division. ... And wherever a true wife comes, this home is always round her.

From J. Ruskin: *Sesame and Lilies* (1905 edn)

B H.G. Wells' fictional heroine is not satisfied with this passive role

[Ann Veronica] wanted to live. She was vehemently impatient - she did not clearly know for what - to do, to be, to experience. And experience was slow in coming. ... The world, she discovered, with these matters barred [i.e. those involving the opposite sex] had no particular place for her at all, nothing for her to do, except a functionless existence varied by calls, tennis, selected novels, walks, and dusting in her father's house. She thought study would be better. She was a clever girl, the best of her year in the high school, and she made a valiant fight for Somerville or Newnham, but her father had met and argued with a Somerville girl at a friend's dinner-table, and he thought that sort of thing unsexed a woman. He said simply that he wanted her to live at home.

From H.G. Wells: *Ann Veronica* (1909)

C V.S. Pritchett recalls his mother's struggle to maintain a respectable existence as the wife of a commercial traveller

It seemed to us that father had genius. By the time there were four children - three boys and a girl - Father seemed as sumptuous as a millionaire and my mother was worn down. It was like a marriage of the rich and the poor. She cooked, cleaned, made our clothes and her own, rarely had the money to pay for a girl to help her and went about a lot of the day with a coarse apron on, her blouse undone and her hair down her back. ... When Father got in he walked into the front room where we ate, sat down in an armchair and, without a word, put out his foot. Mother's duty was to kneel and unbutton his boots until laced boots came in, when she unlaced them; eventually we squabbled for this honour. 'Ease the sock' Father would say with regal self-pity. And he would tell her about the orders he had taken that week. His little order books were full of neat figures and smelled warmly of scent.

From V.S. Pritchett: *A Cab at the Door* (1968)

D WSPU and ILP member Teresa Billington questions marriage itself

Not only has the subjection of women to men been harmful directly and indirectly in the economic world, but it has produced far-reaching evil effects in our social and sex-relations. There is a vital connection between woman's outlawry in industry and her pitiable position of dependence in marriage. Because man desired to keep woman under his control he has denied her the chance of economic independence, he has forced her to feed herself through him. He has done this because he was afraid that if she were free he might lose her. The cloak of marriage has been used to cover unspeakable horrors which women have suffered. Men have known this, and seen the rebellion in women's hearts, and in effect they have said, 'Unless women have no other way of livelihood we shall lose them.' The other alternative - that of removing the evil conditions against which women rebelled, and of making marriage such that they would willingly have entered into it, either never occurred to men's minds or was rejected by them because of the restraint which it entailed for themselves.

From an unpublished manuscript by Teresa Billington: *Woman's Liberty and Men's Fear* (1907)

E   Statistics suggest that in practice women's lives were changing [adapted from various sources]

Birthrate:	1890-1899	30.02 per thousand
	1900-1909	27.50 per thousand

Females over nineteen per thousand:	*1891*	*1901*	*1911*
Unmarried	281	298	302
Married	585	576	579
Widowed	134	126	119

Numbers of women at work:	*1881*	*1911*
Middle-class occupations	427,000	1,114,000
Working-class occupations	2,976,000	3,687,000

Percentage of workers employed:	1881		1911	
	Men	Women	Men	Women
Middle-class occupations	21.5	12.6	25.0	23.7
Working-class occupations	78.5	87.4	75.0	76.3

F   Extracts from George Gissing's novel *The Odd Women*
[Rhoda Nunn explains why she works in a training school for women]
'The pessimists call them useless, lost, futile lives ... I look upon them as a great reserve. When one woman vanishes in matrimony, the reserve offers a substitute for the world's work. True, they are not all trained yet - far from it. I want to help in that - to train the reserve.'
[The school is owned by Mary Barfoot whose aim is] ... to draw from the overstocked profession of teaching as many capable young women as she could lay hands on, and to fit them for certain of the pursuits nowadays thrown open to their sex. She held the conviction that whatever man could do, woman could do equally well - those tasks only excepted which demand physical strength.

From George Gissing: *The Odd Women* (1893)

G   Dr Almroth Wright takes a different view of single women
The recruiting field for the militant suffragists is the million of our excess female population - that million which had better long ago have gone out to mate with its complement of men beyond the sea. Among them there are ... women who have all their life-long been strangers to joy, women in whom instincts long suppressed have in

the end broken into flame. These are the sexually embittered women in whom everything has turned into gall and bitterness of heart, and hatred of men. Their legislative programme is license for themselves, or else restrictions for men. Peace will return when every woman for whom there is no room in England seeks 'rest' beyond the sea ... and when the woman who remains in England comes to recognise that she can, without sacrifice of dignity, give a willing subordination to the husband or father, who, when all is said and done, earns and lays up money for her.

From a letter to *The Times*, 27 March 1912

H   Mrs Pankhurst justifies her militant activities in court
We believe that if we get the vote it will mean better conditions for our unfortunate sisters. Many women pass through this court who would not come before you if they were able to live morally and honestly. The average earnings of the women who earn their living in this country are only 7s and 6d.a week. Some of us have worked for many years to help our own sex, and we have been driven to the conclusion that only through legislation can any improvement be effected, and that the legislation can never be effected until we have the same power as men to bring pressure to bear upon governments to give us the necessary legislation. We have tried every way. We have presented larger petitions than were ever presented before for any other reform, we have succeeded in holding greater public meetings than men have ever had for any reform. ... Because we have done this we have been misrepresented, we have been ridiculed, we have had contempt poured upon us. ... I come here not as an ordinary law-breaker. I should never be here if I had the same kind of laws that the very meanest and commonest of men have - the same power that the wife-beater has, the same power that the drunkard has. This is the only way we have to get that power which every citizen should have of deciding how the taxes she contributes to should be made, and until we get that power we shall be here.

From a speech by Mrs Pankhurst, 1908

I The Polling Station: a poster designed by the Suffrage Atelier (a workshop run by women) for the WSPU, 1912

J A Suffragette's Home: a poster designed by John Hassall for the National League for Opposing Woman Suffrage, 1912

K   Some women still preferred their traditional role

A great question is before the country. It is this: Shall we sacrifice our Womanhood to Politics? Shall we make a holocaust of maidens, wives and mothers on the brazen altars of Party? Shall we throw open the once sweet and sacred homes of England to the manoeuvres of the electioneering agent? Surely the best and bravest of us will answer No! - ten thousand times no! ... For with woman alone rests the Home, which is the foundation of Empire. When they desert this, their God-appointed centre, the core of the national being, then things are tottering to a fall. ... Women's business is to illumine the background - to *inspire* the work, and let her light 'shine through' the victorious accomplishment of noble purpose.

From Marie Corelli: *Woman or - Suffragette? A Question of National Choice* (1907)

L   Winston Churchill opposes the 'Conciliation' Bill which would give the vote only to women who owned property

It is an anti-democratic bill. It gives an entirely unfair representation to property, as against persons. ... What I want to know is how many of the poorest classes would be included? ... The basic principle of this bill is to deny votes to those who are upon the whole the best of their sex. ... This is the new democracy. There is no end to the grotesque absurdities that would follow the passing of this measure. It would be possible for a woman to have a vote while living in state of prostitution; if she married and became an honest woman she would lose that vote, but she could regain it through divorce. ... I cannot conceive why we should be asked to associate ourselves with a measure so ill-conceived in its practical details as this is.

From a speech in the House of Commons, 12 July 1910

M   Labour MP, Philip Snowden, supports the Bill

This question has been before the House of Commons for more than forty years. ... During that forty years women have proved their capacity for public service in a hundred different ways. Women have carried off against men the highest honours the universities can offer, and they have served the State with advantage and honour in many ways. ... The united suffrage organisations of the country demand the enactment of this Bill, not as a favour, but as an act of justice far too long delayed. ... I appeal to the men of this House to rise above political prejudice and masculine bigotry, and to honour themselves by honouring and respecting the womanhood of this nation.

From a speech in the House of Commons, 12 July 1910

N Parliamentary opposition hardened, as the Speaker of the House of Commons explains

The activities of the militant Suffragettes had now [1913] reached the stage at which nothing was safe from their attacks. Churches were burnt, public buildings and private residences were destroyed, bombs were exploded, the police and individuals were assaulted, meetings broken up, and every imaginable device resorted to in order to inconvenience or annoy His Majesty's lieges. ... The feeling in the House, caused by the extravagant and lawless action of the militants, hardened the opposition to their demands, with the result that on the 6th of May the private member's bill, for which the Government had in the previous session promised facilities, was rejected on second reading by a majority of 47.

From Viscount Ullswater: *A Speaker's Commentaries* (1925)

O For Christabel Pankhurst suffrage became a crusade against the scourge of male immorality

Votes for Women and Chastity for Men. ... Regulation of vice and enforced inspection of the White Slaves is equally futile, and gives a false appearance of security which is fatal. Chastity for men - or, in other words, their observance of the same moral standard as is observed by women - is therefore indispensable. Votes for Women will strike at the Great Scourge in many ways. When they are citizens women will feel a greater respect for themselves, and will be more respected by men. They will have the power to secure the enactment of laws for their protection, and to strengthen their economic position. ... For several practical, common-sensible, sanitary reasons women are chary of marriage. ... Mr. Punch's advice to those about to marry - Don't! has a true and terrible application to the facts of the case.

From Christabel Pankhurst: *The Great Scourge and How to End It* (1913)

P In 1914 Sylvia Pankhurst's East London Branch of the WSPU was expelled by her sister, Christabel

Christabel ... announced that the East London Federation of the WSPU must become a separate organisation. ... She added: 'You have a democratic constitution for your Federation; we do not agree with that.' Moreover, she urged, a working women's movement was of no value: working women were the weakest portion of the sex: how could it be otherwise? Their lives were too hard, their education too meagre to equip them for the contest. 'Surely it is a mistake to use the weakest for the struggle! We want picked women, the very strongest and most intelligent!' She turned to me. 'You have your own ideas. We do not want that; we want all our women to take their instructions and walk in step like an army!' ... I was oppressed by a sense of tragedy, grieved by her ruthlessness. Her glorification of autocracy seemed to me remote indeed from the struggle we were waging, the grim fight even now proceeding in the cells.

From Sylvia Pankhurst: *The Suffragette Movement* (1931)

Q   A woman writer explains the movement's failure
The initiative of political reforms was no longer with the people. The days of Reform Bill riots and Chartism had given place to the expert. ... It was one thing to sign a petition or join a suffrage society and quite another to vote against one's party. In those pre-war days every voter in the kingdom might have signed a petition for women's enfranchisement and it would still have been possible for Mr Asquith to lie low and say nothing without the slightest fear of weakening his position.

From Wilma Meikle: *Towards a Sane Feminism* (1916)

R   A feminist historian explains why women gained the vote
Ultimately neither violent nor peaceful acts alone secured women the vote [in 1918]. Suspension of militancy during the war made it easier for politicians to endorse enfranchisement, but the number of changes brought about by the war and the desire of politicians to enlist women's support for post-war reconstruction measures made it prudent to enfranchise most women over thirty years of age. ... Among other things, if women were to support government plans to place returning soldiers in jobs held by women, they had to be co-opted. Limited enfranchisement was the logical means of gulling women into believing that they would at last have the power and the right of making their voice directly heard.

From Suzann Buckley: *The Family and the Role of Women* (1979)

Questions

1   To what extent do the writers of Sources B, C and D and statistics from Source E call Source A into question?   **(6 marks)**

2   Use the statistics from Source E and Sources F and G to explain what was meant in Edwardian times by 'surplus women'.   **(6 marks)**

3   Evaluate the arguments used in Sources H-K.   **(6 marks)**

4   Explain the political motives which lie behind Sources L and M.
(4 marks)

5   In the light of Sources N-R consider the view that the WSPU's militancy harmed the cause of women's suffrage.   **(8 marks)**

8 STRUGGLING OVER IRELAND

In 1904 Edward VII went to see Shaw's new play about Ireland, *John Bull's Other Island,* and laughed so much that he broke his seat. The portly monarch was no doubt amused by the scene in which an Englishman tries to win Irish hearts in an election campaign 'by driving through Rosscullen in a motor car with Haffigin's pig'. But Shaw's intention was to educate as well as to entertain his audience. As an Irishman living in England, he was in a good position to point out to 'John Bull' what he saw as the absurdities of English rule over Ireland. Like one of the characters in his play, Shaw longed for Ireland to be 'a country where the facts are not brutal and the dreams are not unreal' [A].

At the beginning of Edward's reign the Union between Britain and Ireland remained in being, as Gladstone had failed to convince Parliament that the Irish should be allowed to rule themselves. It was the aim of Conservative/Unionist governments to 'kill Home Rule with kindness'. They were certainly prepared to crush any disorder, using methods which caused Balfour to be labelled 'Bloody' during his term as Chief Secretary for Ireland. But their main endeavour was to give loans to help tenants to buy their land and grants to assist the impoverished western districts.

When the Liberals returned to office in 1906 they were more cautious than Gladstone had been. They still supported Home Rule in theory but would only advance towards it, as Sir Edward Grey said, 'step by step'. In their first four years of office they introduced measures to improve Irish housing and education, and set up the National University of Ireland for Roman Catholics. English reforms lessened some Irish grievances. Many small farmers gained the security of owning their own land. Families were glad to move into cottages 'built by the Liberals'. Nevertheless, as early as 1907 it was clear from the protests which destroyed the Liberal Bill to set up an Irish Council to advise the English Lord Lieutenant that Irish nationalists would accept nothing less than Home Rule [B-C].

Most of Ireland could never be happy under English domination. A symptom of discontent was the movement to assert Irish cultural identity. The Gaelic Athletics Association gained widespread support for its rejection of the 'effeminate follies' of English games in favour of hurling and Gaelic football. The Gaelic League sought to 'de-Anglicize' the country by reviving the old language and extolling the qualities of the Irish peasantry. So chauvinist was this organisation that it condemned the work of Anglo-Irish writers like W.B. Yeats and J.M. Synge because, although they concentrated on Irish themes, they did so in the English tongue and did not always idealise their compatriots [D-F].

The intensity of this Anglophobia was demonstrated when Ireland showed sympathy for the Boers during their war with Britain. Two Irish brigades actually fought with the Boers and there were strong protests when Edward VII visited Ireland soon after the war ended. Arthur Griffith was able to tap this hatred as he built up a new independence movement, which became known in 1905 as Sinn Fein ('Ourselves' or 'Our Own Thing'). Rather than work for Home Rule by parliamentary means, Sinn Fein wanted to break all economic and constitutional links with Britain [G-I].

The socialist James Connolly criticised both nationalist and cultural leaders for sentimentalising the past and neglecting the 'present conditions' of Irish peasants and workers, who were among the poorest in Europe. Trade unions in Ireland were as backward as the economy itself until Connolly and James Larkin provided dynamic leadership. As a result Dublin witnessed a wave of strikes between 1911 and 1913, similar to those in mainland Britain. At the same time suffragettes carrying shamrocks marched in Dublin and Belfast. There was, writes Roy Foster, 'a general sense of crisis [in Ireland] during the years before the First World War' [J-K].

The third Home Rule Bill, which aroused extravagant hopes and fears, was at the heart of that crisis. After the two elections of 1910, John Redmond, the leader of the Irish Parliamentary Party, had been able to extract from Asquith a promise that he would introduce Home Rule after placing a veto on the Lords [Chapter 5]. The Bill of 1912 was to establish an Irish Parliament solely responsible for Irish affairs, but answerable to Westminster in matters such as foreign policy, defence and some taxation. Sinn Fein opposed this modest measure. It is not clear whether the Bill would ultimately have satisfied the Irish, for its implementation was prevented by the determination of the north-eastern province of Ulster to preserve the Union. Ulstermen had long argued that their predominant Protestant religion and industrialised economy would suffer if they were governed from Dublin. By this time, they were well organised and had the brilliant barrister, Edward Carson, as their spokesman. Furthermore, the British Conservative Party was also determined to oppose Home Rule, mainly on the grounds that it would break up the Empire [L-N].

During the two years which the Bill took to pass through the Commons three times, and thus become law without the consent of the Lords, events in Ireland made parliamentary debate irrelevant. In 1912, after Bonar Law had announced that his party would support Ulster's defiance whatever lengths it went to, about a quarter of a million Ulstermen swore a Solemn Oath and Covenant to 'use all means' to defeat Home Rule. In the next year they formed an Ulster Volunteer Force which trained openly, at first with wooden rifles and later with weapons smuggled in from Germany. In the spring of 1914 60 British officers at the Curragh army base threatened to resign if they were ordered to crush the Ulster revolt and the Secretary for War, Colonel Seely, assured them that they would not have to. When Asquith heard of this, however, he dismissed Seely and took over the War Office himself. In his ambiguous message to the Curragh officers he said, 'The Army will hear nothing of politics from me and in return I expect to hear nothing of politics from the Army.' Meanwhile, in southern Ireland, nationalists had formed a rival Irish Volunteer Force to fight for Home Rule - or, if Sinn Fein got its way, for a greater measure of freedom. They too became involved in gun-running but, in their case, the authorities did not turn a blind eye. Ireland seemed to be on the brink of civil war [O-Q].

The Liberals were torn between two conflicting principles: should they support Irish national aspirations or should they protect the minority rights of the Protestants? In the end, Asquith sought a compromise. Redmond was persuaded to acquiesce in an amendment allowing some Ulster counties to opt out of Home Rule for a period of six years. This amendment was passed in June 1914. But it was nullified by a further amendment, in the Lords, permanently excluding all the nine counties of Ulster from Home Rule. A special conference at Buckingham Palace failed to find a way out of the impasse and the Bill became law in August with no exclusion clause. When the European war broke out the unworkable Act was suspended. Like Gladstone before him, Asquith had failed 'to pacify Ireland'.

Opinions differ about whether English politicians or the Irish themselves were to blame for this failure. What is certain is that the problems shelved in 1914 were exacerbated by the war. Civil war and partition were all the more bitter when they came and the conflicts of Edwardian Ireland are with us still [R-U].

A Shaw analyses the relationship between Ireland and the English

A conquered nation is like a man with cancer: he can think of nothing else. ... English rule is such an intolerable abomination that no other subject can reach the people. ... A healthy nation is as unconscious of its nationality as a healthy man of his bones. But if you break a nation's nationality it will think of nothing else but getting it set again. It will listen to no reformer, to no philosopher, to no preacher, until the demand of the Nationalist is granted. It will attend to no business, however vital, except the business of unification and liberation. That is why everything is in abeyance in Ireland pending the achievement of Home Rule. ... All demonstrations of the virtues of a foreign govern-ment ... are as useless as demonstrations of the superiority of artificial teeth, glass eyes, silver windpipes, and patent wooden legs to the natural products.

From G.B. Shaw: Preface to *John Bull's Other Island* (1904)

B Balfour explains the purpose behind the 1903 Land Purchase Act
But my honourable friend says - Though the plan may be good in
itself, why is it to be done for these disloyal people? Well, the Bill is
not intended to make people loyal. It is not intended to turn Home
Rulers into Unionists. ... But it is intended to take away one of those
sores which fester and which aggravate every political movement
which might otherwise be innocuous. ... Emotions which are the result
of long generations of ancient and bitter traditions are not easy to blot
out. ... We think that good government and contentment ... ought to
tend and will tend ... to a harmony of feeling between every section
of the community, whether in Ireland, Scotland, or England.

From a speech in the House of Commons, 4 May 1903

C John Redmond rejects the Irish Council Bill of 1907
What they offer us today is not Home Rule; it is not offered to us as
Home Rule; it is offered as a substitute for or an alternative to Home
Rule. ... What we mean by Home Rule is a freely elected Irish
Parliament with an executive responsible to it. What we mean by
Home Rule is that in the management of all exclusively Irish affairs
Irish public opinion shall be as powerful as the public opinion of
Canada or Australia is in the management of Canadian or Australian
affairs. That is our claim; we rest that claim on historic right, on
historic title, but we rest it also on the admitted failure of British
government in Ireland for the last 100 years. ... What has the history
been of your rule? The history of famine, of misery, of insurrection, of
depopulation. ... [But] I say that even if your rule had been as good in
the last 100 years as it has been bad, if it had led to the material
advancement of Ireland ... still our claim would have remained.

From a speech in the House of Commons, 7 May 1907

**D The President of the Gaelic League explains the necessity for
building up an Irish Nation**
But you ask, why should we wish to make Ireland more Celtic than it
is - why should we de-anglicize it at all? I answer because the Irish
race is at present in a most anomalous position, imitating England
and yet apparently hating it. How can it produce anything good in
literature, art, or institutions as long as it is actuated by motives so
contradictory? Besides, I believe it is our Gaelic past which, though
the Irish race does not recognize it just at present, is really at the
bottom of the Irish heart, and prevents us becoming citizens of the
empire. ... What we must endeavour never to forget is this, that the
Ireland of today is the descendant of the Ireland of the seventh

century; then the school of Europe and the torch of learning. ... It has lost all that they had - language, traditions, music, genius and ideas. ... The old bricks that lasted eighteen hundred years are destroyed; we must now set to, to bake new ones, if we can, on other ground and of other clay.

From an address by Douglas Hyde, 25 November 1892

E   The Gaelic Movement disapproved of a young wife's impropriety in a play by J.M. Synge

Tramp: (at the door) Come along with me now, lady of the house, and it's not my blather you'll be hearing only, but you'll be hearing the herons crying out over the black lakes, and you'll be hearing the grouse and the owls with them, and the larks and the big thrushes when the days are warm; and it's not from the like of them that you'll be hearing a tale of getting old ... and losing the hair off you, and the light of your eyes, but it's fine songs you'll be hearing when the sun goes up, and there'll be no old fellow wheezing, the like of a sick sheep, close by your ear.
Nora: You've a fine bit of talk, stranger, and it's with yourself I'll go. *(She goes towards the door, then turns to her husband)* ... What way would a woman live in a lonesome place the like of this place, and she not making a talk with the men passing? *(She goes out with the tramp.)*

From J.M. Synge: *In the Shadow of the Glen* (1903)

F   Yeats defends Synge's play which had been performed at his Irish National Theatre

Literature is always personal, always one man's vision of the world, one man's experience, and it can only be popular when men are ready to welcome the vision of others. A community that is opinion-ridden, even when those opinions are in themselves noble, is likely to put its creative minds into some sort of prison. If creative minds preoccupy themselves with incidents from the political history of Ireland, so much the better, but we must not enforce them to select those incidents. [He protests against a public imagination which is] ... full of personified averages, partisan fictions, rules of life that would drill everybody into the one posture, habits that are like the pinafores of charity schoolchildren.

Fellow-nationalist, Maud Gonne, is not prepared to compromise
Mr Yeats asks for freedom for the theatre, freedom from patriotic captivity. I would ask for freedom for it from one thing more deadly than all else - freedom from the insidious and destructive tyranny of foreign influence.

From letters to *The United Irishman,* 10, 17 and 24 October 1903

G A French postcard of 1900 suggests that the Empire is causing Britain nothing but trouble

H   An Irish Home Rule postcard of 1908 [Old Ireland is symbolised by the round tower, the wolfhound and the emigrant ship, while the boy and the rising sun represent hopes for the future]

"Ireland Sings her Old Songs"

HOME RULE

I   Arthur Griffith argues for economic independence

We in Ireland have been taught by our British lords lieutenant ... that our destiny is to be the fruitful mother of flocks and herds - that it is not necessary for us to pay attention to our manufacturing arm, since our agricultural arm is all sufficient. A merely agricultural nation can never develop to any extent a home or foreign commerce, increase its population in due proportion to their well-being or make notable progress in its moral, intellectual, social and political development; it will never acquire important political power or be placed in a position to influence less advanced nations and to form colonies of its own.

We must offer our producers protection where protection is necessary. ... If an Irish manufacturer cannot produce an article as cheaply as an English or other foreigner, solely because his foreign competitor has had larger resources at his disposal, then it is the duty of the Irish nation to accord protection to the Irish manufacturer.

From a speech to the first Annual Conference of Sinn Fein, 28 November 1905

J Historian F.S. Lyons selects details from reports on Dublin between 1908 and 1914

About thirty per cent (87,000) of the people of Dublin lived in the slums which were for the most part the worn-out shells of Georgian mansions. Over 3,000 families lived in single-room tenements which were without heat or light or water (save for a tap in a passage or backyard) or adequate sanitation. Inevitably, the death-rate was the highest in the country, while infant mortality was the worst ... in the British Isles. Disease of every kind, especially tuberculosis, was rife and malnutrition was endemic; it was hardly surprising that the poor, when they had a few pence, often spent them seeking oblivion through drink. ... Most slum families seem to have earned less than a pound a week in 1909 and virtually all of this went on the barest necessities of life.

From F.S. Lyons: *Ireland Since the Famine* (1971)

K In his autobiography the playwright Sean O'Casey describes the attitudes of his fellow building labourers

Not one of these brawny boys had ever heard of Griffith or of Yeats. They lived their hard and boisterous life without a wish to hear their names. A good many of them had done seven years' service in the British Army, and now served on the Reserve, for sixpence a day wasn't to be sneezed at. What to them were the three Gaelic candles that light up every darkness: truth, nature, and knowledge. Three pints of porter, one after the other, would light up the world for them. If he preached the Gaelic League to any one of them, the reply would probably be, Aw, Irish Ireland me arse, Jack, not makin' you an ill answer, oul' son. What would the nicely-suited, white-collared respectable members of the refined Gaelic League branches of Dublin do if they found themselves in the company of these men? Toiling, drinking, whoring, they lived everywhere and anywhere they could find a ready-made lodging or room. ... And yet Sean felt in his heart that these men were all-important in anything to be done in Ireland.

From Sean O'Casey: *Drums under the Windows* (1945)

L Asquith explains the limited nature of Home Rule

We maintain in this Bill unimpaired, and beyond the reach of challenge or of question, the supremacy, absolute and sovereign, of the Imperial Parliament. The powers which we propose to give to Ireland of taxation, of administration, of legislation, are delegated powers, but within the limits of that delegation they embrace at once, with the exception of the reserved services, all matters of local concern. If, as we believe will be the case ... power carries with it a sense of responsibility that will give to the Irish people a free and ample field for the development of their own national life and at the same time bind them to us and the Empire by a sense of voluntary co-operation, and, as I believe, in sincere and loyal attachment. ... There has been reserved for this Parliament ... the double honour of reconciling Ireland and emancipating herself.

From a speech in the House of Commons, 11 April 1912

M From the Census of 1911

	Protestant	Catholic	Total
Ulster	891,000	691,000	1,582,000
Three southern provinces	250,000	2,550,000	2,800,000
Whole of Ireland	1,141,000	3,441,000	4,382,000

But not all the counties of Ulster contained a Protestant majority

	Protestant	Catholic
Antrim	79.0%	20.5%
Down	68.4%	31.6%
Armagh	54.7%	45.3%
Londonderry	54.2%	45.8%
Tyrone	44.6%	55.4%
Fermanagh	43.8%	56.2%
Monaghan	25.3%	74.7%
Donegal	21.1%	78.9%
Cavan	18.5%	81.5%

N Kipling expresses the Unionists' extreme hatred for Catholic Ireland

We know the war prepared
On every peaceful home,
We know the hells declared
For such as serve not Rome -
The terror, threats, and dread
In market, hearth, and field -
We know, when all is said,
We perish if we yield.

From Rudyard Kipling: 'Ulster 1912'

O Conservative leader, Bonar Law, stands by the Ulstermen

The Chief Liberal Whip has told us that the Home Rule Bill will be carried through the House of Commons before Christmas. Perhaps it will. I do not know. But I do know this - that we do not acknowledge their right to carry such a revolution by such a means. We do not recognise that any such action is the constitutional government of a free people. We regard them as a revolutionary committee which has seized by fraud upon despotic power. In our opposition to them we shall not be guided by the considerations ... which would influence us in any ordinary political struggle. ... We shall use any means to deprive them of the power they have usurped and to compel them to face the people they have deceived. Even if the Home Rule Bill passes through the House of Commons, what then? I said in the House of Commons, I repeat here, that there are things stronger than Parliamentary majorities.

From a speech made at a rally at Blenheim Palace, 29 July 1912

P Sir Edward Carson explains why Ulster rejects Home Rule
Let us leave out the sentiment of the matter altogether. ... How will Ulster be better under the Bill? ... What single advantage will Ulster get under the Bill? ... She will be degraded from her position in this House, and she will be put into a perpetual minority in the House in Dublin, and the great and expanding industries in the North of Ireland will be at the mercy and governed, by whom? ... Some three or four hundred thousand small farmers with the labourers attached, in the South and West of Ireland, with whom they have nothing whatsoever in common, either in ideal or objects, or race or religion, or anything that makes up a homogeneous nation. ... In Belfast, at all events, and in some of the larger towns around it, you are dealing with men who have to engage in great businesses, and you have given us in this Bill the rottenest finance that has ever been proposed in this House. ... There is nothing in the Bill that ... can improve the material condition of Ulster.

From a speech in the House of Commons, 1 January 1913

Q John Redmond rejects the principle of exclusion
This Home Rule question is for us the demand of a nation for the restoration of its national rights. ... Ireland for us is one entity. It is one land. Tyrone and Tyrconnell are as much a part of Ireland as Munster or Connaught. Some of the most glorious chapters connected with our national struggle have been associated with Ulster. Our ideal in this movement is a self-governing Ireland in the future, when all races and creeds within her shores will bring their tribute, great or small, to the great total of national enterprise and national statesmanship and national happiness ... [Exclusion] would for all time mean the partition and disintegration of our nation. To that we as Irish Nationalists can never submit.

From a speech in the House of Commons, 1 January 1913

R Asquith's biographer defends the Prime Minister's record
Asquith's relative inactivity on Ireland during the sessions of 1912 and 1913 had more to commend it than is commonly allowed. Additional action beyond the trundling of the Bill round parliamentary circuits might easily have made matters worse. Furthermore, for a Government which appeared to be beset on all sides ... and which faced a

constant series of parliamentary crises, a certain massive calmness on the part of its head was by no means a negligible asset. ... He remained calm, detached and mildly optimistic. When confronted with apparently insoluble crises he consoled himself with his 'fixed belief', as he wrote to Venetia Stanley [his confidante], 'that in politics the expected rarely happens.'

From Roy Jenkins: *Asquith* (1964)

S Another historian attacks Asquith

Asquith's failure [to carry Home Rule] was all the more tragic in that he missed one of the best opportunities history has ever offered for the peaceful solution of the Ulster problem. ... [He] rejected the appeal of Lloyd George and Churchill that special provision be made for Ulster in the 1912 Bill ... and failed to seize the opportunity for dealing with Ulster on his own terms. ... The Cabinet did not treat Ulster's resistance seriously until autumn 1913, when it was far too late to avert the growing crisis. ... Compromise might have been possible before the two sides became so intransigent. ... Asquith relied throughout on a high-risk policy of prevarication and delay ... and total deadlock was reached several months before the European war broke out. ... Asquith lacked Gladstone's boldness and generosity in relation to Ireland. Caution and procrastination were not effective substitutes.

From Patricia Jalland: *The Liberals and Ireland* (1980)

T His biographer reminds us that Bonar Law was an Ulsterman

[Bonar Law] deeply felt the character of the measure which would put his fellow-countrymen under the rule of their hereditary enemies in Southern Ireland. He really believed that a Dublin Parliament would ruin Belfast, that the liberties of the Ulstermen would vanish, that a prosperous enlightened community would be subjected to intolerable treatment at the hand of Southern bigots, that it was an outrage to drive out from their allegiance to the Crown a population which was so clearly determined to be loyal. Thinking like this - whether rightly or wrongly does not matter - he was bound to regard as legitimate almost any means of destroying the Home Rule Bill.

From R. Blake: *Bonar Law: The Unknown Prime Minister* (1955)

U An Irish historian takes a less sympathetic view

The electoral situation reinforced Tory convictions. The Conservatives had been out of office for seven years by 1912, the longest consecutive period in half a century that their leaders had been deprived of the privilege of displaying their devotion to the national interest at the highest level. They sniffed a winning issue in 'the Empire in danger'. ... Bonar Law claimed that Home Rule had not been a special election issue in 1910. Therefore the Liberals had no mandate to implement it. ... Bonar Law's demand for a general election on this issue was brilliantly opportunistic. ... But what if the Liberals were to win the next general election? ... Bonar Law left himself an escape route from inconvenient electoral verdicts. He spattered his demands for a fresh appeal to the electorate with the reassurance that 'there are things stronger than parliamentary majorities'.

From J.J. Lee: *Ireland 1912-1985* (1989)

Questions

1 How far do Sources A-C explain why the Irish demand for Home Rule was not 'killed with kindness'? **(6 marks)**

2 What different conceptions of Irish history and culture are illustrated in Sources D-H? **(6 marks)**

3 Compare the usefulness of Sources I-K for learning about economic conditions in early twentieth-century Ireland. **(5 marks)**

4 Use Sources L-Q to summarise the arguments for and against Home Rule for the whole of Ireland. **(8 marks)**

5 Discuss, with reference to Sources R-U, the extent to which English politicians can be blamed for the failure of Home Rule. **(5 marks)**

9 DESCENDING INTO WAR

When Austrian troops were moved to the Serbian border on 25 July 1914 and European war threatened, Asquith wrote: 'This will take the attention away from Ulster, which is a good thing.' However, historians do not suggest that the government entered 'this hateful war' as a way of resolving domestic problems. On the contrary, it feared that the hardships of war would increase the danger of revolution. When the army was sent to the Continent in August, two divisions were kept back to deal with British rioters as well as with German invaders. So, why did Liberal ministers, many of whom had passionately opposed the Boer War, decide to involve Britain in this dangerous conflict?

The story begins with the loss of confidence caused by the Boer War. Isolation was no longer 'splendid'. To defend the Empire in future Britain clearly needed to strengthen her armed forces and to find allies. Both the Conservative Foreign Secretary, Lord Lansdowne, and his Liberal successor, Sir Edward Grey, pursued these aims.

Annual defence spending increased during Edwardian years from £35 million to £91 million. Between 1903 and 1909 Britain's defences were augmented by a General Staff to act as the army's 'brain', an Officers' Training Corps in the public schools, a force of part-time Territorial soldiers and a British Expeditionary Force of 150,000 men, ready to fight overseas. But, alone among European powers, Britain did not introduce conscription, an unpopular idea despite the propaganda of the National Service League. After all, the navy was the country's first line of defence and Britannia still ruled the waves. In order to preserve this supremacy, especially over the growing German fleet, the energetic First Sea Lord, Admiral Fisher, introduced a new type of battleship in 1905 - the Dreadnought. It was so large, fast and well-armed that it rendered all other warships obsolete. As Germany continued to expand her navy, Britain responded by building more Dreadnoughts as well as smaller battle-cruisers and submarines. By 1914 Britain was still in the lead [A-E].

This naval rivalry rendered futile attempts at an Anglo-German alliance such as those made by Joseph Chamberlain in 1899 and 1901. After the Boer War ended, Lansdowne set out to forge other links, while trying hard to keep his distance from both of the existing European armed camps: the Triple Alliance between Germany, Austria and Italy; and the Dual Alliance between France and Russia. The alliance he signed with Japan in 1902 reduced Britain's naval commitment in the Far East. To avoid becoming involved in the approaching war between Japan and

Russia, Britain then negotiated a friendly agreement with France (Russia's ally). The further aim of this 1904 Entente was to settle old colonial scores; in return for French recognition of British rule in Egypt, Britain secretly agreed to support French claims in Morocco. This promise, historians can now see, had unforeseen repercussions [F].

Jealous of the large empires already possessed by Britain and France and wanting 'a place in the sun' for Germany, the Kaiser challenged French rights over Morocco in a speech at Tangier in 1905. At the ensuing Algeçiras Conference Grey, who had just become Foreign Secretary, supported the French. He went on to hold military talks with France. Not even the Cabinet was told of these 'conversations' and no formal record was kept. Grey always insisted that they were 'non-committal', but the French now understood that British armed assistance might, in future circumstances, be forthcoming [G-H].

Still pursuing his predecessor's policy of cautious rapprochement, Grey formed an Entente with Russia in 1907. This agreement, too, resolved old imperial conflicts. Again, a friendship treaty which looked innocent enough had the effect of heightening Anglo-German tension. Germany had been 'encircled', the Kaiser cried. He blamed his British cousin, Edward VII (said by historian Samuel Hynes to be the only modern monarch deserving to be called 'a good European'), for his visits had eased the way for both Ententes. Further German naval expansion prompted the Cabinet to build eight more Dreadnoughts, the expense of which helped to provoke the Budget crisis of 1909.

A second Moroccan crisis in 1911 revealed the dangerous state of European relations. Germany sent a gunboat, the *Panther,* to the port of Agadir as a protest against the presence of French troops in Morocco. Grey interpreted this as a challenge to the Entente and gave strong support to France. In the general alarm, even Lloyd George, who had been a leading exponent of non-aggressive principles in the Liberal Party, pronounced that peace should not be purchased at the cost of 'national honour'. Further Anglo-French naval talks were held, in which it was secretly agreed that British ships should safeguard the North Sea and Channel, allowing the French to move their vessels to the Mediterranean. In 1912 Germany had to recognise Morocco as a French protectorate. As compensation the Kaiser received land in the Congo.

Meanwhile, radical and socialist MPs had bitterly attacked the Foreign Secretary for his 'secretive' and 'provocative' diplomacy. He was able to ride out the storm but modified his policies slightly in response to these criticisms. In the next couple of years he was more conciliatory towards Germany. The two countries were even able to mediate together to end the Balkan wars of 1912 and 1913. 'The spring and summer of 1914', wrote Winston Churchill in 1938, 'were marked in Europe by an exceptional tranquillity' [I].

Little though the public was allowed to know about all this high diplomacy, there was no lack of interest in foreign affairs. A few newspapers, like the *Daily News* and the *Nation* regularly expressed opinions similar to those of Grey's parliamentary critics. Norman Angell's *The Great Illusion,* an exposure of the absurdity of war, was reprinted ten times between 1910 and 1914. Labour leaders urged the working class to reject the idea of fighting their proletarian brethren abroad. Yet, even in the socialist movement there were those, like Robert Blatchford, who warned of the German menace and argued for national service. Such views were much more widespread than idealistic pacifism. The public eagerly lapped up a stream of articles, novels and plays telling of imminent German invasion and omnipresent alien spies. Many newspapers joined the *Daily Mail* in calling for conscription and faster naval expansion. The public schools inculcated manly patriotism and this was more widely disseminated among the country's youth through textbooks, comics and the Boy Scout Movement. All this helped to create a climate of opinion which made war glamorous and acceptable; nevertheless, it cannot be argued that Britain went to war in 1914 by public demand. In any case, Grey's aristocratic background and elevated position meant that he had little contact with the media, let alone the masses [J-N].

Neither the British people nor the government saw the assassination in Sarajevo of the heir to the Austrian throne by a Bosnian Serb nationalist as a cause for Britain to become involved in war. For the next few weeks during that hot summer of 1914 Grey worked hard for a peaceful solution, urging Germany to restrain her ally, Austria-Hungary, from extreme action against Serbia. When this failed and Germany gave Austria her unconditional support, Russia came to Serbia's aid and war between the two alliances ensued between 1 and 3 August. But Britain still had 'no commitment'. Grey felt passionately that Britain could not stand by, seeing her national interests threatened and facing a 'miserable and ignoble future'. He was not, however, sure of Cabinet support until 2 August, when he persuaded most ministers that the understandings reached over the last ten years obliged Britain to give France naval support if the German fleet entered the Channel. Germany's threatened invasion of neutral Belgium provided moral justification for war. After his speech in the Commons on 3 August, Grey was acclaimed by most MPs of all parties, including the Irish Nationalists - though two members of the Cabinet resigned in protest (as did the Labour leader, MacDonald, who deplored his colleagues' support for the war). To judge by the 'tremendous cheering' which greeted the declaration of war on 4 August and the speed with which men and women of all classes volunteered for service, Grey had also convinced the British public. But few foresaw the bitter ordeal awaiting those who marched off to fight for King and Country [O-T].

A A collection of General Roberts' speeches became a bestseller

I give place to no man in my admiration for, and my belief in, our
Navy, but it seems to me little short of madness to suppose that the
Navy will always, and under all circumstances, be able to prevent the
invasion of these Islands, or to secure the defence of the Empire. We
must have, in addition, a suitable Army, and this we shall never get
until the whole nation realises that it is the duty of every able-bodied
citizen to fit himself to take his share in the defence of his country. ...
It is because I fear that nothing short of national disaster will make
the people of this country realise this - for long years of immunity
from home trouble have engendered a feeling of security which has
no justification at the present day, and have induced a taste for ease
and luxury to which everything must give way, and which causes the
calls of duty to be felt as an intolerable interference with their
pleasure and recreation - it is because of this fear that I so earnestly
press for the boys and youths of Great Britain to be given an
education which will teach them their duty to their country, and imbue
them with that spirit of patriotism without which no nation can expect
to continue great and prosperous.

From Lord Roberts: *A Nation in Arms* (1907)

B Robert Graves recalls the patriotism at his public school

One of my last recollections at Charterhouse [in summer 1914] is a
school debate on the motion 'that this House is in favour of compulsory military service'. The Empire Service League, with Earl Roberts of
Kandahar, V.C., as its President, sent down a propagandist in support.
Only six votes out of one hundred and nineteen were noes. I was the
principal opposition speaker, having recently resigned from the
Officers' Training Corps in revolt against the theory of implicit
obedience to orders. ... Of the six noes, Nevill Barbour and I are, I
believe, the only ones who survived the war. ... At least one in three
of my generation at school died; because they all took commissions
as soon as they could, most of them in the infantry and Royal Flying
Corps.

From R. Graves: *Goodbye to All That* (1929)

C George Gissing describes the feelings of ordinary schoolboys

Someone, I see, is lifting up his sweet voice in praise of Conscription.
... I am happy in believing that most English people are affected by it
even as I am, with the sickness of dread and of disgust. ... Let
England be imperilled, and Englishmen will fight; in such extremity
there is no choice. But what a dreary change will come upon our
islanders if, without constant danger, they bend beneath the curse of
constant soldiering! I like to think that they will guard the liberty of
their manhood even beyond the point of prudence. ... At school we

used to be 'drilled' in the playground once a week; I have but to think of it, even after forty years, and there comes back upon me that tremor of passionate misery which, at the time, often made me ill. ... To be sure, nearly all my schoolfellows either enjoyed the thing, or at all events went through it with indifference. ... Even of those who, boylike, enjoyed their drill, scarce one or two, I trust, would have welcomed in their prime of life the imposition of military servitude upon them and their countrymen.

From G. Gissing: *The Private Papers of Henry Ryecroft* (1903)

D   The relative strength of the British and German Forces in 1914 [adapted from various sources]

	Britain	Germany
Army divisions	8	50
Reserve divisions	28	32
Dreadnoughts	20	13
Battle-cruisers	8	5
Older battleships	40	22
Cruisers	58	7
Destroyers	300	144
Submarines	78	28

E   A Grand Review of the Fleet before George V at Spithead on 17-18 July 1914

F King Edward VII (sometimes known as 'Edward the Caresser') visits Paris in 1903

When England ... decided to patch up old quarrels with France, Edward's talents as *Roi Charmeur* smoothed the way. ... For four days he made appearances, reviewed troops at Vincennes, attended the races at Longchamps, a gala at the Opera, a state banquet at the Quai d'Orsay and, at the theatre, transformed a chill into smiles by mingling with the audience in the *entr'acte* and paying gallant compliments in French to a famous actress in the lobby. Everywhere he made gracious and tactful speeches about his friendship and admiration for the French, their 'glorious traditions', their 'beautiful city' ... his 'sincere pleasure' in the visit, his belief that old misunderstandings are 'happily over and forgotten', that the mutual prosperity of France and England was interdependent and their friendship his 'constant preoccupation'. ... Within a year, after hard work by ministers settling disputes, the rapprochement became the Anglo-French Entente.

From Barbara Tuchmann: *August 1914* (1962)

G Grey's confidential account of his talks with the French Ambassador

Monsieur Cambon, in summing up what I had said, dwelt upon the fact that I had expressed my personal opinion that, in the event of an attack by Germany upon France, no British Government could remain neutral. I said that ... much would depend as to the manner in which war broke out between Germany and France. I did not think people in England would be prepared to fight in order to put France in possession of Morocco. ... But if, on the other hand, it appeared that the war was forced upon France by Germany to break up the Anglo-French 'Entente', public opinion would undoubtedly be very strong on the side of France. At the same time, Monsieur Cambon must remember that England at the present moment would be most reluctant to find herself engaged in a great war. ... I asked Monsieur Cambon, however, to bear in mind that, if the French Government desired it, it would be possible at any time to re-open the conversation.

From a despatch to Sir F. Bertie, the British Ambassador in Paris, 31 January 1906

H Even Lloyd George was 'kept in the dark'

There is no more conspicuous example of this kind of suppression of vital information than the way in which the military arrangements we entered into with France were kept from the Cabinet for six years. ... There is abundant evidence that both the French and the Russians regarded these military arrangements as practically tantamount to a commitment on our part to come to the aid of France in the event of her being attacked by Germany. ... And yet the Cabinet were never informed of these vital arrangements until we were so deeply involved in the details of military and naval plans that it was too late to repudiate the inference.

From David Lloyd George: *War Memoirs* (1934)

I   A Liberal MP attacks Grey's policies

The foreign policy of the Government is not a Liberal foreign policy. It is not merely a continuation, but it is an accentuation of the foreign policy of our predecessors. We have this question of the balance of power raised to a sort of fetish which the whole of the Foreign Office staff and the Foreign Secretary as well worship, and our foreign policy seems to feed the balance of the scales with slices of the Congo or of Morocco. When it is not a question of the balance of power the one other thing that seems to affect our Foreign Office policy is that of material British interest. ... We have a genuine right to say to Liberal Ministers, we expect broad Liberal principles to be followed. ... I say that the majority of Englishmen place the moral results of our foreign policy above the material results, and that they are more anxious for justice between foreign nations than they are for commercial treaties or extra concessions in Africa or Asia or Arabia. ... It is about time the people of England and Germany insist upon knowing what it is these diplomatists are playing at. They are playing, not a national game, but merely a plutocratic financial game. It is a game, not of national honour, but of national dishonour.

From a speech in the House of Commons by J. Wedgewood, 14 December 1911

J   An extract from Norman Angell's widely read pacifist tract

[England must take the lead] in one of those great moral and intellectual movements which would be so fitting to her leadership in such things as human freedom and parliamentary democracy. Failing such effort and such responsibility, what are we to look for? ... Are we to continue to struggle, as so many good men struggled in the first dozen or so centuries of Christendom - spilling oceans of blood, wasting mountains of treasure - to achieve what is at bottom a logical absurdity; to accomplish something which, when accomplished, can avail us nothing, and which, if it could avail us anything, would condemn the nations of the world to never-ending bloodshed and the constant defeat of all those aims which men, in their sober hours, know to be alone worthy of sustained endeavour?

From N. Angell: *The Great Illusion* (1910)

K The *Daily Mail* commissioned a novel about a German invasion of Britain as part of its scaremongering campaign
The exact whereabouts of the enemy was not known. They were, it seemed, everywhere. They had practically overrun the whole country, and the reports from the Midlands and the North showed that the majority of the principal towns had now been occupied. The latest reverses in London, full and graphic accounts of which were now being published hourly by the papers, had created an immense sensation. Everywhere people were regretting that Lord Roberts' solemn warnings had been unheeded, for had we adopted his scheme for universal service such dire catastrophe could never have occurred. ... The repeated warnings had been disregarded, and we had, unhappily, lived in a fool's paradise, in the self-satisfied belief that England could not be successfully invaded.

From R. le Queux: *The Invasion of 1910* with a Preface by Lord Roberts (1906)

L The *Observer* urges the building of more Dreadnoughts
By an act of moral treachery, which would justify us in armed reprisals now, a foreign Power has doubled its naval programme, in secret, and has gained six months' start in a conspiracy against our life. ... Let us keep our dignity. Let us keep our heads. Insist on the Eight, the whole Eight and nothing but the Eight, with more to follow, and break any man or faction who stands in the way.

From *The Observer*, 21 March 1909

M The radical *Daily News* denounces this 'outcry'
Panic, always infectious, is spreading like the plague ... a horrible and dangerous phenomenon. As an extreme example, take the sort of maddened apprehension under which the *Observer* was shivering yesterday. ... It betrays every evidence of terror and excitement. ... What we complain of is the scurrilous abuse poured upon a great nation with whom we are, nominally, at all events, on terms of peace and friendship.

From the *Daily News*, 22 March 1909

N   Meanwhile the Boy Scouts keep a keen look-out for the enemy

Part I.   Price 4d. net

SCOUTING FOR BOYS BY B-P

(LIEUT. GEN.
BADEN POWELL C.B.

PUBLISHED BY HORACE COX,
WINDSOR HOUSE, BREAM'S BUILDINGS, LONDON E.C.

O Grey finally reveals Britain's inescapable obligations
The French fleet is now in the Mediterranean, and the Northern and Western coasts of France are absolutely undefended ... because of the feeling of confidence and friendship which has existed between the two countries. My own feeling is that if a foreign fleet engaged in a war which France has not sought ... came down the English Channel and bombarded and battered the undefended coasts of France, we could not stand aside and see this going on practically within sight of our eyes, with our arms folded, looking on dispassionately, doing nothing! ... But I also want to look at the matter without sentiment, and from the point of view of British interests. ... [If] the French fleet is withdrawn from the Mediterranean ... consequences would be forced upon us because our trade routes in the Mediterranean might be vital to this country. ... What is our position in regard to Belgium? ... We have great and vital interests in the independence ... of Belgium. ... If, in a crisis like this, we run away from those obligations of honour and interest as regards the Belgian Treaty, I doubt whether, whatever material force we might have at the end, it would be of very much value in face of the respect we should have lost. ... I have put the vital facts before the House. ... When the country realises what is at stake, what the real issues are, the magnitude of the impending dangers in the West of Europe ... we shall be supported throughout, not only by the House of Commons, but by the determination, the resolution, the courage, and the endurance of the whole country.

From a speech in the House of Commons, 3 August 1914

P Ramsay Macdonald rejects the Foreign Secretary's arguments
I am convinced that this war ... is no people's war. It is a war that has been made ... by men in high places, by diplomatists working in secret, by bureaucrats who are out of touch with the peoples of the world. ... I want to make an appeal on behalf of the people, who are voiceless except in this House, that there should be a supreme effort made to save this terrible wreckage of human life, that we may not make further sacrifice upon the altar of the terrible bloodstained idol of the balance of power, but should be willing to make great sacrifices of patience in the sacred cause of peace.
Keir Hardie adds a threat
The decision of the Government has been come to without consulting the country. ... I say respectfully to the House that some of us will do all we can to rouse the working classes of the country in opposition to this proposal of the Government. ... A few years hence, and if we are led into this war, we shall look back in wonder and amazement at the flimsy reasons which induced the Government to take part in it.

From speeches in the House of Commons, 3 August 1914

Q For many upper-class women like Joan Poynder the war provided a chance to work

The war changed everybody. ... When I was sixteen ... I had this passion for independence you see and I knew that I wasn't going to get much in the pre-war days except through marriage. But it wasn't necessarily a thing that one wanted to do at once. But luckily I got it immediately by pretending I was much older and going in for nursing. Which nobody could stop me doing. My generation was pretty well wiped out.

From T. Thompson: *Edwardian Childhoods* (1981)

R For young men war often meant the chance to live more intensely, as Julian Grenfell affirms a few months before his death on the Western Front

... he is dead who will not fight;
  And who dies fighting has increase.

The fighting man shall from the sun
  Take warmth, and life from the glowing earth;
Speed with the light-foot winds to run,
  And with the trees to newer birth;
And find, when fighting shall be done,
  Great rest, and fullness after dearth.

From 'Into Battle' by J. Grenfell, eldest son of Lord Desborough (1915)

S J.B. Priestley, a middle-class Bradford boy, recalls a sense of adventure

I went at a signal from the unknown. ... There came, out of the unclouded blue of that summer, a challenge that was almost like a conscription of the spirit, little to do with King and Country and flag-waving and hip-hip-hurrah, a challenge to what we felt was our untested manhood. Other men, who had not lived as easily as we had, had drilled and marched and borne arms - couldn't we? Yes, we too could leave home and soft beds and the girls to soldier for a spell, if there was some excuse for it, something at least to be defended. And here it was.

From J.B. Priestley: *Margin Released* (1962)

T A blacksmith from Suffolk explains why he volunteered

There were about eight from this village killed. ... We all went to the war, me and the other boys ... I listed directly arter the war bruk out ... and went into the Huss Artillery. ... I was cheerful - we all were. We called it the 1914 spirit. Everybody wanted a goo in that war. They all fared to want to join in, like. Us 1914/1915 boys volunteered. I am glad I went; I'm proud of it and no mistake. We used to sing a song that went somethin' like this, 'How will you fare in the old man's chair' if you don't have a go? ... I got cut-up a good bit too, but I wouldn't ha' missed it, that I wouldn't! As God's my Maker I wouldn't ha' missed it, cut-up an' all.

From R. Blythe: *The View in Winter* (1979)

Questions

1 In the light of Sources A-E how would you have advised the Liberal government on the issue of conscription?   **(5 marks)**

2 Compare the usefulness of Sources F-H in explaining Britain's relations with France between 1904 and 1911.   **(6 marks)**

3 What different approaches to foreign and defence matters are illustrated in Sources I-N?   **(7 marks)**

4 Evaluate the arguments used by Sir Edward Grey and his opponents in Sources O and P.   **(7 marks)**

5 To what extent do Sources Q-T illuminate what the Suffolk blacksmith calls 'the 1914 spirit'?   **(5 marks)**

10 ESTIMATING THE EDWARDIAN AGE - THE HISTORICAL DEBATE

This chapter includes different views of the Edwardian age which have been adopted by memoir writers and historians. The extracts illustrate three continuing and closely-linked debates.

1. Was the Liberal Party (which was in power for most of this period) already in a state of irreversible decline?

2. Should the Edwardian era be remembered as a harmonious 'golden age' or as a time of harsh social contention?

3. Was the Edwardian age part of modern times or does the First World War form the great divide?

1 Was the Liberal Party in a state of irreversible decline?

This debate was initiated in the 1930s by George Dangerfield. He argued that the Liberal Party was mortally wounded by the rivalry of the new Labour Party, the unconstitutional activities of the Conservatives and the violent rebellions of the workers, the Irish and the suffragettes. He highlighted three symbolic moments: the debate on the Miners' Minimum Wage in March 1912; the Curragh Mutiny in March 1914; and the suffragette bomb in May 1914. Dangerfield's dramatic version was not challenged until 1966 when Trevor Wilson argued that these difficulties merely suggest that the Liberal party was ailing, but not doomed. This interpretation did not convince Labour historians like Ross McKibbin, who argued that the crucial factor was the growth of the trade unions and their affiliation with the Labour Party. Revisionist historians have since argued that Liberal decline was not inevitable before the First World War - indeed the party was in a powerful position. But the debate continues.

A Dangerfield's three symbolic moments
The Debate on the Miners' Minimum Wage

'We have exhausted all our powers of persuasion and argument and negotiation,' Asquith concluded, in low thick halting tones. 'But we claim to have done our best in the public interest - with perfect fairness and impartiality.' He stood there, struggling for words; and they would not come. The House watched him, fascinated and appalled: something was taking place before its eyes which not one of its members had expected to see. The Prime Minister was weeping. ... Those tears ... seem more and more like a tragic confession, not merely of a personal failure, but of the failure of Liberalism itself.

The Curragh Mutiny

Not since 1688, when James II lost his crown, had the Army refused to obey its orders, as it now refused to obey them; not since 1688 had it controlled the country: this was the first time since that violent year, that an Opposition had promoted a rebellion, and the first time in all history that a Liberal Government virtually ceased to govern.

The Suffragette Bomb

[As the Home Secretary Reginald McKenna spoke in the Commons MPs heard] a muffled explosion from the direction of Westminster Abbey. A suffragette bomb had gone off beneath the Coronation Chair. ... Thunder itself could not have been more appropriate. 'Patient and determined action' - against these words, with their familiar, their fatal Liberal ring, the heavens themselves might have uttered their voice. The situation had passed far beyond the control of Mr McKenna. ... Mr Asquith and his Cabinet gave up the battle.

From G. Dangerfield: *The Strange Death of Liberal England* (1935)

B Trevor Wilson challenges Dangerfield's version

[These difficulties merely suggest] that the Liberals would lose the next election to the Conservatives. ... They do not show that it was doomed to near-extinction. ... The social reforming wing of the Liberal government was making the running. 'Advanced' thinkers were still looking to Liberalism to implement their ideas. And Labour had put forward no major policy items which the Liberal Party was unable to implement. ... There was domestic unrest, but no anarchy. ... The Liberal Party can be compared to an individual who, after a period of robust health and great exertion, experienced symptoms of illness (Ireland, Labour unrest, the suffragettes). Before a thorough diagnosis could be made, he was involved in an encounter with a rampant omnibus (the First World War), which mounted the pavement and ran him over. After lingering painfully, he expired. A controversy has persisted ever since as to what killed him.

From T. Wilson: *The Downfall of the Liberal Party* (1966)

C Labour historians like Ross McKibbin were not convinced

[The crucial factor was] the nature of the relationship between the Labour Party and the trade-unions on the one hand, and between the trade-unions and the industrial working-classes on the other. Since the Labour Party was inextricably linked to the unions, it ... gained electorally from their growth [and also from] a heightening class-consciousness in the industrial working-class. ... The eclipse of the Liberal Party ... was not due to 'the war', or a wrong-headed pursuit of *laissez-faire,* or the split between Asquith and Lloyd George [during the war], or the conversion of the workers to socialism, but to a slow change in the way popular political affiliations were decided. As political allegiance became more and more determined by class self-awareness, the Liberal Party found that it could make no claim on the loyalties of any class.

From R. McKibbin: *The Evolution of the Labour Party* (1974)

D   A revisionist historian argues that the Liberals still occupied a significant position in pre-war politics
The Cabinet's reforming coalition of New Liberals and Centrists was still intact. The New Liberals were preparing to push the party still further to the left. ... The ability to evolve towards new goals, and embrace a variety of appeals, helped the Liberal party hold traditionally Liberal, but socially mixed, rural/middle-class seats, at the same time that its major support came from industrial areas. ... There was an important potential problem: Labour expansion. ... [But at this stage] Labour's positive appeal was so localised (and so complementary to that of the Liberal Party) that co-operation between parties sharing similar goals was pragmatically sensible. ... There were few signs that the Progressive Alliance was collapsing in 1914, rather more that Labour was under considerable stress. As party leaders recognised, the Liberals were in a powerful position.

From D. Tanner: *Political Change and the Labour Party* (1990)

E   A recent article finds this argument 'inconsistent'
A more balanced approach is necessary which accepts that the First World War was responsible for significant political and social change but admits that the Liberal Party was finding great difficulty in containing Labour's pre-war challenge. ... It is clear that the process of political change was well established before the First World War. Local research combines with national evidence to suggest that a powerful Labour Party had emerged with MPs, rising trade-union membership and increasing financial support. ... On the eve of war the Labour Party was well established and threatening the hegemony of the Liberal Party in progressive politics. ... The problem for the Liberal Party was that its neglect of labour interests had been evident for more than three decades before the 1924 general election [in which the Liberals gained only forty seats] and that its perception of this failing had come too late for it to recapture the left.

From K. Laybourn: 'The Rise of Labour and the Decline of Liberalism' in *History* (June 1995)

2 Should the Edwardian era be remembered as a 'golden age'?

This section views the Edwardian age through the memories of those who lived at that time.

F An American heiress who married into English High Society

We went to our first Garden Party in the grounds of Windsor Castle. It remains in my memory as one of the loveliest of the Royal Garden Parties. The ladies of that time dressed beautifully in flowing summer dresses with flower-trimmed hats and lacy parasols. They no longer have the time or the leisure to be as beautiful as they were in the early days of this century. ... We enjoyed ourselves light-heartedly, and loved every minute of our lives. In retrospect, the summers seem to have been real summers then - the river always sparkling in the sunlight, the sky always blue. ... The shadows of this century had not yet fallen across our lives. The 1914 War, with all its horrors, had yet to come.

From the Marchioness Curzon of Kedleston: *Reminiscences* (1955)

G Harold Nicolson mixed in similar circles

Who among us today would really dress for church and dress for luncheon and dress for tea and dress again for dinner? Who among us would possess the endurance to relish all those meals, to relish all that tittle-tattle? Who today would care whether he was or was not invited to Upyatt Lacy or to West Warren? Who today prints or reads those lists of Saturday to Monday parties? The war has not been fought in vain. We have been released from false and exacting pretensions.

From H. Nicolson: *Small Talk* (1937)

H Edmund Blunden, son of a village schoolmaster

The reign of King Edward seemed, in spite of some occasional nonsense (my German cousin, not altogether gently, had said there was to be a war between our nations), a golden security. Everything did: the *Daily Telegraph,* the fishmonger on his due hour once a week with his basket on his imperial head (Mr Goodwin), the flower show, and the never-delayed 2.23 to Maidstone on Saturday afternoon. The ripened apple-orchards and the light smoke from the September hop-kilns were always there. Perhaps the innovation of the magic lantern service in our old church did not please everybody, but Mr Brooker and his bell-ringers did. Now I come to think of it, Mr Brooker and our Brigadier-General on the old Western Front had much the same gift of leadership.

From E. Blunden: 'Country Childhood' in *Edwardian England,* edited by S. Nowell-Smith (1964)

I   Robert Graves, son of a school inspector
At the age of four and a half I caught scarlet fever and ... my parents sent me off to a public fever hospital. The ward contained twenty little proletarians, and only one bourgeois child besides myself. I did not notice particularly that the nurses and my fellow-patients had a different attitude towards me; I accepted the kindness and spoiling easily, being accustomed to it. But the respect and even reverence given to this other little boy, a clergyman's child, astonished me. 'Oh,' the nurses would cry after he had gone, 'he did look a little gentleman in his pretty white pelisse when they took him away!' 'That young Matthew was a fair toff,' echoed the little proletarians. On my return from two months in hospital, my accent was deplored, and I learned that the boys in the ward had been very vulgar. I did not know what 'vulgar' meant; it had to be explained to me. About a year later I met Arthur, a boy of nine, who had been in the ward and taught me how to play cricket when we were convalescent together. He turned out to be a ragged errand-boy. ... I suddenly realised with my first shudder of gentility that two sorts of Christians existed - ourselves, and the lower classes.

From R. Graves: *Goodbye to All That* (1929)

J   V.S. Pritchett recollects his father's clothing business
[His] customers were the wealthy and overfed Edwardians who were just about to be impoverished by the war - their very houses looked overfed with hangings, bric-a-brac and cushions - who lived choleri-cally [irritably] and almost untaxed, on their means. They were above all a race who draped themselves. I was puzzled when I saw the Sunday processions of unemployed marching with their banners and when I thought of my father's struggles in his trade; and now when I read books of nostalgia about Edwardian times, I find I remember nothing but the English meanness. ... The war changed everything. The stuffed, quilted and cushioned Edwardian age had gone; the age so soft for the bottoms of the comfortably off, so mean and bitterly exacting for the struggling, small man, so wretched for the poor.

From V.S. Pritchett: *A Cab at the Door* (1968)

K   Clifford Hills, whose family lived 'from hand to mouth'
One thing as a boy I didn't like and it sticks in my mind today. I came to the conclusion that church-goers were something like the railway carriages were at one time - first, second and third class. You see my mother was a person of the lower class, she was a poor woman, and ... her friends were all poor, but they were great church-goers, kindly,

gentle people. But they had to sit in the back pews. In the middle of the church were the local shopkeepers and people who were considered to be a little bit superior to the others, better educated perhaps. And right at the top of the church ... were the local farmers, the local bigwigs, you see, posh people. And when people left the church, although he was a nice kindly vicar, he didn't seem to have any time for the lower classes. Mother and her friends would pass out of the church door ... and he would just nod and smile, perhaps not that even. But when the higher-class people came out he would shake hands and beam to every one of them as if they were somebody far superior to my mother. ... And I didn't like that. I thought my mother was worth a handshake as well as the rich.

From T. Thompson: *Edwardian Childhoods* (1981)

L Fred Mitchell, a poor Suffolk labourer

I never did any playing in all my life. There was nothing in my childhood, only work. I never had pleasure. One day a year I went to Felixstowe along with the chapel women and children, and that was my pleasure. But I have forgotten one thing - the singing. There was such a lot of singing in the villages then, and this was my pleasure, too. Boys sang in the fields, and at night we all met at the Forge and sang. The chapels were full of singing. When the first war came, it was singing, singing all the time. So I lie; I have had pleasure. I have had singing.

From R. Blythe: *Akenfield* (1969)

M A village Post Office in Dorset - 'Paradise Lost'?

3 Was the Edwardian era part of modern times?

N Virginia Woolf claimed that 'human character changed' in 1910. Some historians agree

An assault on the Edwardian imagination had been launched by the Post-Impressionist exhibition in London at the end of 1910, organised by Roger Fry. The conventional art public was at first shocked by what it took to be either a bad joke or attempted fraud, but the exhibition was influential in beginning the break-up of old attitudes too long continued. ... By 1914 Post-Impressionism had been followed from the Continent by Cubism, Futurism and other innovations. Painters like Matisse and Picasso, composers like Debussy and Stravinsky, a ballet dancer such as Nijinsky ... represented an often aggressive new approach in the arts. 'Advanced' opinion responded first and most consciously to these new stimuli, but by 1914 even ordinary Edwardian men (and women) had begun to widen the limits of what they accepted as proper and possible both in the arts and in human relationships. Serge Diaghilev, the ballet impresario and an open homosexual, was lionized by Edwardian society only some fifteen years after Oscar Wilde had been imprisoned and ostracized for much less public activity.

From D. Read: *Edwardian England* (1972)

O The teenage J.B. Priestley enters the modern world in 1911

One evening [in Leeds], hot and astonished in the Empire, we discovered ragtime, brought to us by three young Americans. ... It was as if we had been living in the nineteenth century and then suddenly found the twentieth glaring and screaming at us. We were yanked into our own age, fascinating, jungle-haunted, monstrous. We were used to being sung at in music-halls in a robust and zestful fashion, but the syncopated frenzy of these three young Americans was something quite different; shining with sweat, they almost hung over the footlights, defying us to resist the rhythm, gradually hypnotising us, chanting and drumming us into another kind of life in which anything might happen. ... Out of those twenty noisy minutes in a music-hall, so long ago, came fragmentary but prophetic outlines of the situation in which we find ourselves now, the menace to old Europe, the domination of America, the emergence of Africa, the end of confidence and any feeling of security, the nervous excitement, the frenzy, the underlying despair of our century.

From J.B. Priestley: *Margin Released* (1962)

P   Writer G.K. Chesterton sees special significance in the Marconi scandal of 1912. [Lloyd George and other ministers were accused of using inside knowledge to purchase shares in the Marconi Company when it was just about to receive a government contract to build a chain of radio stations]

It is the fashion to divide recent history into Pre-War and Post-War conditions. I believe it is almost as essential to divide them into the Pre-Marconi and Post-Marconi days. It was during the agitations upon that affair that the ordinary English citizen lost his invincible ignorance, or, in ordinary language, his innocence. ... The pivotal fact of the position, of course, was that ... the very extraordinary monopoly which the Government then granted to the Marconi Company was in fact granted to its managing director, Mr Godfrey Isaacs, the brother of Sir Rufus Isaacs, then the Attorney General [a Cabinet Minister]. ... Until the editor of the *Eye-Witness* [Chesterton's brother, Cecil] forced the politicians to reveal something, they had begun by protesting that there was nothing whatever to reveal. [In the end a Parliamentary inquiry exonerated the ministers but Lloyd George's reputation was tarnished.]

From G.K. Chesterton: *Autobiography* (1936)

Q   Another memoir plays down the importance of pre-war change

It was an age of increasing speed. The motor-car and the motor-omnibus had arrived. In 1909 an aeroplane flew the Channel for the first time. The moving picture began its bewildering onslaught on the human consciousness. ... The modern newspaper was launched, disseminating news with increasing rapidity ... The telephone was increasing the tempo of human contact. ... But the first appearance of an invention is not the moment of its general impact. We must not exaggerate the extent of these inventions in the Edwardian Age. Rather they were a source of wonder and of belief in uninterrupted progress than a wide influence on existence. The Edwardian Age was nearer in its daily life to the Age which preceded it than to the Age which followed.

From W.S. Adams: *Edwardian Portraits* (1957)

R   Historian R.C.K. Ensor was one of the young Edwardian men

[... who] felt themselves at the beginning, not at the end, of an age. It was to be an age of democracy, of social justice, of faith in the possibilities of the common man. ... To sum up these immediate pre-war years, it may be said, so far as England is concerned, that most of the familiar post-war tendencies were already developing in them. The war altered direction less than is often supposed. It accelerated changes ... but they were germinating before it. It may be that some would have been carried through more wisely but for the war's revolutionary atmosphere. It may be, on the other hand, that an undistracted concentration upon home issues would itself have bred some kind of revolution - a view to which the pre-war loss of balance about home rule lends a certain colour. All that is now a matter of speculation. What is not, is the seething and teeming of this pre-war period, with its immense ferment and its restless fertility.

From R.C.K. Ensor: *England 1870-1914* (1936)

S Philip Larkin's poem was inspired by photographs of crowd scenes at the outbreak of the war

Those long uneven lines
Standing as patiently
As if they were stretched outside
The Oval or Villa Park,
The crowns of hats, the sun
On moustached archaic faces
Grinning as if it were all
An August Bank Holiday lark;
And the shut shops, the bleached
Established names on the sunblinds,
The farthings and sovereigns,
And dark-clothed children at play
Called after kings and queens,
The tin advertisements
For cocoa and twist, and the pubs
Wide open all day;

And the countryside not caring:
The place-names all hazed over
With flowering grasses, and fields
Shadowing Domesday lines
Under wheat's restless silence;
The differently-dressed servants
With tiny rooms in huge houses,
The dust behind limousines;
Never such innocence,
Never before or since,
As changed itself to past
Without a word - the men
Leaving the gardens tidy,
The thousands of marriages
Lasting a little while longer:
Never such innocence again.

Philip Larkin: 'MCMXIV' (1957)

T   This may be one of the photographs which inspired Larkin

Questions

1 In the light of Sources A-E, explain whether you think the Liberal Party was already doomed by 1914.   **(8 marks)**

2 Use Sources F-M (or others in the book) to discuss what we have gained and lost since Edwardian times.   **(8 marks)**

3 With reference to Sources N-R discuss what you consider to be the most modern aspect of the Edwardian age.   **(6 marks)**

4 To what extent do Sources S and T convince you that there was an 'innocence' before the First World War?   **(5 marks)**

5 Select from this chapter one extract which romanticises the Edwardian age, one which is neutral, and one which deplores it. Explain briefly the reason for each choice.   **(3 marks)**

11 DEALING WITH EXAMINATION QUESTIONS

Specimen Answers to Source-based Questions

Questions based on Chapter 3 - ('Improving the Youth' see pages 26-36).

Questions

1   In the light of Sources A-E discuss the view that the Edwardian era was a 'golden age' for children.   **(7 marks)**

2   Compare the suggestions for improving 'national efficiency' made in Sources F-J and assess their practicality.   **(7 marks)**

3   How useful are Sources K and L in illustrating the opportunities for secondary education after the 1902 Act?   **(6 marks)**

4   How valid, in the light of Sources M-O, are the objections made in Source P to the Liberal reforms concerning children?   **(6 marks)**

5   In what ways might the child in Source R be said to live up to the ideals contained in Source Q?   **(4 marks)**

Points to note about these questions

1   This question asks you to discuss a rather general statement. You can use the sources freely here to form your own impressions. You do not have to come to a definite conclusion.

2   It is important here to compare the sources and to comment on the suggestions made in them. Were they sensible and practical? Would contemporaries have found them acceptable? What do they tell us about the authors' assumptions?

3   You need to concentrate particularly here on the provenance, date and bias of the sources. Do they support or contradict each other?

4   The strong statement made in Source Q can be compared to the more neutral evidence contained in the other sources.

5   This is just a simple comparison, but it may tell you something about Edwardian times.

will not help people to 'raise themselves', which remains current today.

5 In what ways might the child in Source R be said to live up the ideals contained in Source Q?   **(4 marks)**

There is no reference in Source R to whistling and singing - though Emma seems to be cheerful enough despite her difficult circumstances. In other ways she conforms admirably, though unwittingly, to Baden-Powell's ideals (Q); she is extremely 'useful', dutiful, obedient and 'thrifty'. She does not, of course, have much opportunity to be 'a snob' or to look down on others, since she lives at the bottom of society. It is most unlikely that a child like Emma would have been able to afford either the money or the time to become a Girl Guide. The two sources illustrate in an oblique way the great gulf fixed between the upper and lower classes in Edwardian times.

Preparing Essay Answers

As the reports of the examination boards point out year after year, the greatest single weakness among examinees is an inability to be relevant in their answers. No matter how well read and knowledgeable candidates may be, if they stray too far from the terms of the question they cannot be given credit. Examinations from A level upwards are basically a test of the candidates' ability to analyse historical material in such a manner as to present a reasoned, informed response to a specific question. Too often examiners are faced with regurgitated notes on a set of topics, little of which relates to the questions as set. There is really no such animal as an 'easy' exam question at these levels; those who set the papers seldom repeat the exact wording of previous questions. This means that each question demands its own individual interpretation. The intelligence and subtlety of the candidates' response will determine how high a mark they score. Examinees must, of course, have 'knowledge', but academic history tests not only what they know but how well they use what they know. As an aid to the development of effective examination technique, here is a list of questions that candidates should ask themselves when preparing their essays:

1 *Have I answered the question* AS SET or have I simply imposed my prepared answer on it?

2 *Have I produced a genuine argument* or have I merely put down a number of disconnected points in the hope that the examiners can work it out for themselves?

3 *Have I been relevant in arguing my case* or have I included ideas and facts that have no real relation to the question?

4 *Have I made appropriate use of primary or secondary sources to illustrate my answer?*

5 *Have I tried to show originality* or have I just played safe and written a dull, uninspired answer?

Possible Essay Titles

1 Why, and with what results, did the Labour Party emerge as a political force from 1900 to 1914?

The first part of the essay should explain the formation of the Labour Representation Committee in 1900 and weigh up the different factors: the influence of Keir Hardie and the ILP, socialist ideals, the growing power of the trade unions and the Taff Vale case. The electoral performance of the new party and its influence on the Liberal government after 1906 should then be assessed. Finally, it is important to question the extent to which Labour was a political force before 1914 - did it pose a real threat to the Liberals?

2 Account for the decisive defeat of the Conservatives in 1906.

The Conservatives had been in power for most of the last twenty years, due partly to the Liberal split over Home Rule (which gave them the support of Liberal Unionists) and partly to the imperialist mood of the country. By 1906, however, the Liberals had been able to unite in the face of a Tory Party which was itself now divided over Chamberlains's Tariff Reform campaign. This was the main election issue but others should be discussed: the difficult last stages of the Boer War, the use of cheap Chinese labour in South Africa and the controversial Education Act of 1902. The trade unions and the new Labour Party also played an influential part in determining the election result.

3 To what extent were the social reforms of the Liberals between 1906 and 1914 inspired by fear of the Labour Party?

This is a question about the origins of the Liberal reforms and time should not be wasted in explaining the rise of the Labour Party. Fear of being replaced as the party of the left was undoubtedly one influence behind the Liberal reform programme. But other motives should be considered: the shocking revelations of Booth and Rowntree, fears about national efficiency, 'New Liberal' theories and the genuine reforming zeal of ministers.

4 How successful were the Liberals in dealing with the problems of poverty and need in the years from 1906 to 1914?

This question requires some detail about the reforms passed by the Liberals. The Children's Charter, old age pensions, the trade boards, labour exchanges and the National Insurance scheme should all be examined carefully in the light of this question. It is important to reveal the limited nature of the measures and to mention the continuation of the workhouse system. Did the Liberals lay the foundations of the modern welfare state or not?

5 Why, and with what results, did the House of Lords challenge the Liberal government in 1909?

Although the question mentions 1909, it is necessary to show that the Lords had been using their power against the Liberal government since 1906. In view of this and the mounting insecurity felt by the landed classes, it is not difficult to explain the Lords' rejection of Lloyd George's radical 1909 Budget, the terms of which should be briefly mentioned. It is worth discussing whether the Liberals deliberately planned a conflict which would enable them to curb the Lords. The obvious result was the Parliament Act but other consequences should be shown: Balfour's resignation, the weakened position of the Liberals after the 1910 elections, their dependence on the Labour and Irish Parties - and the introduction of the Home Rule Bill so dreaded by the Unionists. The great political significance of this conflict should be emphasised.

6 Why was the period from 1909 to 1914 one of political and social conflict?

The aim of this essay should be to analyse the reasons behind the many conflicts in this period: Lords and Conservatives versus the government, trade unions versus employers and the government, suffragettes versus men and the government, Ulster Unionists and Conservatives versus Liberals and Irish Nationalists. Was there anything in common between these struggles? Were they symptoms of what Samuel Hynes calls 'a conflict between old and new ideas'?

7 Assess the effectiveness of the attempts made by British governments between 1901 and 1914 to deal with the problems of Ireland.

This essay should first describe the still unsolved problems of Ireland (religious divisions, insecure land tenure and dislike of English rule). The Conservative/Unionist and early Liberal policy of 'killing Home Rule with kindness' (far-reaching economic reform from an authoritarian government) should then be considered. Although the land problem was now much alleviated, the continued demand for self-government forced the Liberals to introduce the third Home Rule Bill of 1912. Religious divisions now came to the fore and frustrated the Liberals' last pre-war attempt to solve the problems of Ireland.

8 'It was the First World War, rather than the activities of the suffragettes, that gained women the vote.' Do you agree?

This essay requires not only a knowledge of the suffragette movement, but also some grasp of the vital wartime role of women - in recruitment, employment, nursing and the armed forces. The main point is to discuss why the vote was granted in 1918. There are several controversial questions to consider. How important were the activities of the constitutional suffragists? Was the militant suffragette campaign counter-productive or did it ensure that politicians could no longer ignore the women's cause? Was the vote a consolation prize for women who had to give way to men at the end of the war?

9 Discuss the view that Lloyd George was the inspiration behind the successes of the Liberals from 1906 to 1914.

What were the successes of the Liberals? Their social reforms, the People's Budget, the Parliament Act, and their intervention in some labour disputes can all be counted as such. In all of these Lloyd George played a crucial role - in drafting legislation, in brilliant speeches, in parliamentary struggles, in influencing colleagues and in the clever conciliation of opponents. Also, he had further plans for land reform which might have led to more success had war not intervened. But other people and other factors were important, too. Campbell-Bannerman, Asquith and Churchill were active supporters of reform and much was owed to non-parliamentarians like Rowntree and to socialist ideas. Thus Lloyd George was not the only inspiration, vital though he was. It is also the case that he incurred mistrust by his involvement in the Marconi scandal and by his vacillating attitudes over foreign policy.

10 What interests justified Britain's entry into the First World War in August 1914?

The essay could begin with the idea that Britain went nobly to war for the sake of Belgium and then go on to show that its own interests were also at stake. Britain's emergence from isolation should be explained in terms of the need to defend the Empire. The French Entente, with its secret agenda of mutual defence arrangements, is crucial here. The Russian Entente, which led to German fears of encirclement, should also be discussed. Britain's rivalry with Germany - economic, imperial and naval - should form a central theme of the essay. The conclusion could well quote from Grey's speech of 3 August in which he explained the interests which meant that Britain could not 'stand aside' from the conflict.

Specimen Essay Answer

(See especially Chapters 6, 7, 8 and 10)

> How far were Liberal policies from 1906 responsible for the unrest faced by the government from 1909 to 1914?

Most historians agree that the Liberal Party was sick in 1914, though not all support Dangerfield's contention that it was dying. This question implies that, like the degenerate males castigated by Christabel Pankhurst, the Liberals brought disease on themselves. Was this really the case or were the Liberals scourged by ills which were not of their own making? Why did workers, women and Ulstermen launch such vehement, and often violent, attacks between 1909 and 1914?

One early Liberal policy which could be held responsible for the great increase in industrial action after 1910 is the Trade Disputes Act of 1906. In restoring to strikers the full protection of the law, the Act fulfilled the Liberals' election pledge to reverse the Taff Vale decision. Most Liberals actually believed in the workers' right to strike and they thus opened the door to labour unrest. Furthermore their cautious social policies, which failed to eliminate poverty, disappointed the working class. On the other hand, the strikers did not come from the ranks of the very poor - it was the somewhat better-paid workers who went on strike after 1910.

A more obvious cause of industrial troubles was the government's delay in reversing the Osborne judgement of 1909 and restoring the unions' right to support the Labour Party. While most Liberals agreed that this should be done (even though it would help their political opponents), their preoccupation with Irish Home Rule and Welsh Disestablishment meant that the Trade Union Act was not passed until 1913. Keith Laybourn goes so far as to blame the Liberals' difficulties with the unions on their long 'neglect of labour interests'; other historians claim that their readiness to send troops in to deal with strikers exacerbated the situation. However the Liberal government cannot be held responsible for the stagnation in real wages, the flaunting of wealth by the upper classes, the growth of the Syndicalist movement and the unreasonable behaviour of some employers - all of which helped to cause pre-war strikes.

Women, as well as trade unions, had high hopes that the new Liberal government would redress their grievances. There had been much talk during the 1906 election of franchise reform and many candidates had promised to grant the vote to women. It is not surprising that suffragists protested when this was not done. Asquith was especially culpable here; his aloof distaste for the cause meant that private members' bills to extend the vote to women foundered, as did the Conciliation Bill of 1910. It was even suspected (probably unjustly) that he persuaded the Speaker to withdraw the Franchise Bill of 1913 rather than have females included in it. Other Liberal ministers, like Lloyd George, Churchill and Grey, were more sympathetic in principle. But they hesitated to support limited female suffrage schemes for fear of damaging Liberal electoral fortunes.

Thus, by inaction rather than by deliberate policy, the Liberal government caused frustration and anger among women. Whether it actually provoked the Pankhursts' campaign of violence is debatable. Some historians argue that militant suffragettes made it increasingly difficult for the WSPU's potential supporters in the government to espouse the cause. It is also worth remembering that female suffrage had many opponents outside Parliament, including large numbers of women. The Liberals were not solely responsible for this form of unrest.

Even more serious than these two crises was the simultaneous threat of civil war in Ireland. In this instance, too, the Liberals committed sins of omission, in that they did not take up Gladstone's Home Rule banner during their first four years of office. Instead, they introduced useful measures to improve Irish housing and education. They also tried in vain to set up a virtually powerless Irish Council. The Liberals knew, of course, that Home Rule would not get through the Lords and they were not prepared at this stage to face the contentious issue of House of Lords reform. However, once they had passed the Parliament Act in 1911, they had no excuse to delay Home Rule any longer. Anyway, the close results of the 1910 elections made them dependent on the Irish Nationalist Party. In this way they created their own sea of troubles.

What wrecked the Home Rule Bill of 1912 was the rebellion (rather than the 'unrest') of the Ulstermen. They refused, on economic, religious and, some would say, 'racist' grounds, to be part of a self-governing Ireland. In trying to satisfy the demands of most Irish people for self-determination, the government had ignored the interests of the Protestant minority. Two liberal principles were at odds and the Liberal Party could not implement both. Some argue that Asquith should have anticipated this dilemma and put in an exclusion clause from the beginning. Others say that he should have stood up to the Ulster Unionists more firmly. Instead he relied, as Patricia Jalland says, on 'prevarication and delay' and last-minute compromises which were acceptable to no one. In the end he was relieved when the outbreak of war took 'the attention away from Ireland'. There is no doubt about the Liberals' failure but it was by no means all their own fault. The intransigence of both sides in Ireland and the Conservative Party's cynical encouragement of Ulster's armed rebellion overwhelmed them.

In each case unrest was self-generated but it was aggravated by Liberal policies, as well as by the high expectations aroused when they took power after so many years of Tory rule. Was this period of revolt, perhaps, inevitable? The sway of the upper-class English male was bound to be challenged eventually and the challenges were likely to come when a less repressive party came to power. Liberals believed, as George Bernstein says, in 'an ideology of moderation, reason and restraint'. By their very nature they were peculiarly unable to deal with intransigent opponents who, for various reasons, rejected 'liberal virtues'. It was, indeed, their virtues as much as their vices which made the Liberals prone to the ills which assailed them in the years before the First World War.

BIBLIOGRAPHY

One of the best ways to understand the mentality of Edwardians is to read what they wrote themselves. You could follow up some of the contemporary novels, plays, poetry and surveys quoted in this book. The following list contains some of the most readable social and political histories of the period.

Jane Beckett and Deborah Cherry: *The Edwardian Era* (Phaidon Press and Barbican Art Gallery 1987). Published to accompany an exhibition, this contains interesting visual material and some unusual perspectives on the period.

Keith Benning: *Edwardian Britain* (Blackie 1980). A short survey of the controversial areas, illustrated with source material.

Ronald Blythe: *Akenfield: Portrait of an English Village* (Allen Lane 1969). The interviews with the older people of the village vividly recall the early years of this century.

Piers Brendon: *Eminent Edwardians* (Secker & Warburg 1979). Irreverent portraits of Mrs Pankhurst, Balfour, Baden-Powell and Lord Northcliffe.

Harry Browne: *The Rise of British Trade Unions* (Longman 1979). The later chapters with their accompanying documents are very useful.

Lawrence Butler and Harriet Jones: *Britain in the Twentieth Century: A Documentary Reader* (Heinemann 1994). The first four chapters contain good source material on this period, which could be followed up in the later chapters.

George Dangerfield: *The Strange Death of Liberal England* (Paladin 1970). A stimulating and controversial narrative of the last four troubled years of the period.

R.C.K. Ensor: *England 1870-1914* (OUP 1936). The authoritative Oxford history, written by an Edwardian.

Joe Finn and Michael Lynch: *Ireland and England 1789-1922* (Hodder & Stoughton 1995). Reviews the major aspects of this difficult relationship, with stimulating written and visual sources.

Roy Foster: *Modern Ireland 1600-1972* (Penguin 1989). The interested reader can study the origins and the results of the Irish crisis in this scholarly work.

Jose Harris: *Private Lives, Public Spirit: Britain 1870-1914* (Penguin 1994). A detailed and up-to-date social history of late-Victorian and Edwardian England.

Samuel Hynes: *The Edwardian Turn of Mind* (Princeton/OUP 1968). A most stimulating history of Edwardian ideas and culture.

Michael Lynch: *Lloyd George and the Liberal Dilemma* (Hodder & Stoughton 1991). A short biography which takes up the key issues in a controversial career.

Simon Nowell-Smith (ed): *Edwardian England* (OUP 1964). Well-written essays on a wide range of topics, including music, sport and science.

Alan O'Day (ed): *Edwardian England: Conflict and Stability* (Macmillan 1979). Eight stimulating essays on major themes.

J.B. Priestley: *The Edwardians* (Heinemann 1970). A well-illustrated and lively account.

Donald Read: *Edwardian England* (Harrap 1972). An indispensable study of the period, full of fascinating detail.

Donald Read: *Documents from Edwardian England* (Harrap 1973). A companion volume, containing a wide variety of sources.

Donald Read (ed): *Edwardian England* (Croom Helm & Historical Association 1982). A selection of essays by experts on different aspects of the period.

Donald Read: *The Age of Urban Democracy: England 1968-1914* (Longman 1994). A clear and well-written textbook, recently revised.

Keith Robbins: *The Eclipse of a Great Power: Modern Britain 1870-1975* (Longman 1983). A useful, wide-ranging textbook, with an excellent compendium of information.

Paul Thompson: *The Edwardians: The Remaking of British Society* (Routledge 1992). Written by a pioneer of oral history, this book is based on the life stories of some 500 Edwardians.

Paul Thompson and Gina Harkell: *The Edwardians in Photographs* (Batsford 1979). A most evocative collection.

Thea Thompson: *Edwardian Childhoods* (Routledge & Kegan Paul 1981). A fascinating series of interviews which spans the social spectrum.

INDEX